GANGS

Trouble in the Streets

Marilyn Tower Oliver

—Issues in Focus—

ENSLOW PUBLISHERS, INC.

44 Fadem Road   P.O. Box 38
Box 699   Aldershot
Springfield, N.J. 07081   Hants GU12 6BP
U.S.A.   U.K.

To my dear husband, Floyd, who was always there for me with encouragement, enthusiasm, and love.

Library of Congress Cataloging-in-Publication Data

Oliver, Marilyn Tower.
      Gangs : trouble in the streets / Marilyn Tower Oliver.
         p. cm. — (Issues in focus)
      Includes bibliographical references and index.
      ISBN 0-89490-492-2
1. Gangs—United States—Juvenile literature. 2. Juvenile delinquency—United States—Prevention—Juvenile literature. 3. Violence—United States—Juvenile literature. [1. Gangs.] I. Title. II. Series: Issues in focus (Springfield, N.J.)
      HV6439.U5045   1995
      364.1'06'0973—dc20   94-34619
                                       CIP
                                       AC

Printed in the United States of America

10 9 8 7 6 5 4 3 2

Illustration Credits: Ernest Archuleta, Colorado Department of Corrections, p. 95; Boys & Girls Clubs of America, p. 52; California Department of Corrections, pp. 93, 102; Crime in the United States, Uniform Crime Reports, pp. 79, 80, 81; Buddy Fowler, Los Angeles County Sheriff's Department, p. 76; The Jacob A. Riis Collection #141, Museum of the City of New York, p. 62; Library of Congress, pp. 12, 15, 17, 21; National Institute of Justice, U.S. Department of Justice, pp. 30, 34, 39, 45, 83; Marilyn Tower Oliver, pp. 27, 37, 51, 55, 66, 68, 99.

Cover Illustration: Marilyn Tower Oliver

Contents

Acknowledgments

The author would like to thank the following for their time and assistance in helping research this book:

- ◆ Tammy Membreno, executive director of the Barrio Action Group, Los Angeles
- ◆ Dr. Jennifer Friday, Center for Disease Control, Atlanta
- ◆ Paul Jones, Community Youth Gang Services, South Central Los Angeles
- ◆ Sergeant Wesley McBride, Operation Safe Streets, and Officer George Ducoulombier, Sheriff's Department Information Bureau, Los Angeles Sheriff's Department
- ◆ Mark Lutin and William B. Kearney, Boys and Girls Clubs of America
- ◆ Children's Club, Assistance League of Southern California
- ◆ Office of Tipaton Kindell, California State Department of Corrections

I would also like to thank my family for their patience, understanding, and support of this project.

1

Gangs Are a Serious National Problem

Brenda Harris, age seventeen, made a fatal mistake. When she thought she saw a friend in a passing car, the Tacoma, Washington, teenager waved. Four local gang members who were affiliated with the Crips, a Los Angeles-based street gang, interpreted her wave as a hand signal of the Bloods, a rival gang.

As the driver pulled alongside Brenda's car, two young men leaned out of the windows, and a third stood up through the sunroof, shooting at her with a shotgun, a rifle, and a pistol. She died instantly.[1]

◆　　◆　　◆　　◆

Lamoun Thames, fifteen, dreamed that one day he would play professional football. Every morning he would wake up at 5:30 A.M. to catch a school bus and ride thirty-five miles from his home in South-Central Los Angeles to a suburb in the San Fernando Valley. During the summer of 1992 he took city buses to go to his high school for preseason football practice in hopes of making the varsity team. One August evening, he was stabbed to death while waiting for the bus that would take him home. Although the murderers thought he was a member of a rival gang, there was no evidence that Lamoun was a gang member.[2]

◆　　◆　　◆　　◆

Anthony Gallivan, an immigrant from Ireland, went for dinner with friends at a Chinese restaurant in Elmhurst, Queens. While they were waiting to be served, they noticed that two well-dressed Chinese boys were arguing with the manager. The argument escalated into violence. In the shooting that followed, Gallivan was shot. The bullet passed through his heart, killing him.

The boys who killed Gallivan were members of a vicious Chinese gang that was involved in racketeering and extortion. (Extortion is demanding money with the threat of violence if refused.)[3]

The Gang Problem

Street gangs are not a new phenomenon in America. They existed in large cities in the nineteenth century. In some gangs, such as the Latino gangs of the Southwest which started in the 1920s, membership can span generations. Gangs come from every ethnic group. Although many people are more familiar with African-American and Hispanic gangs, there are gangs in almost all ethnic groups.

The number of gang members is astounding. In 1991, there were an estimated 130,000 gang members in Los Angeles County (population 8,776,000). These ranged from subteen "peewees" to as many as 13,000 hard-core killers. In 1990, gangs in Los Angeles County accounted for 18,059 violent felonies and 690 deaths. Every ethnic group was represented—black, white, Asians, Pacific Islanders, Jewish, and Armenian.[4]

Gangs are a problem in cities large and small. A study by the University of Southern California Center for Research on Crime and Social Control found that street gangs operate in 94 percent of all major cities in the United States and can be found in at least 1,130 cities of all sizes.

In the past, most youth gangs were active in the poor neighborhoods of large urban cities. Although gang activity is still greater in the inner city, today's gang members are mobile and take their violence to parts of the city or suburbs far from their home turf. Suburbs also have their own gangs.

Gang members can be seen in suburban malls. In Los Angeles, members from two rival gangs fired shots at one another in the Westwood Pavilion, an upscale mall, endangering shoppers who happened to be nearby.

Gang Violence Affects Everyone

Even if you are never involved with a gang or the violence gangs cause, you and your parents will pay the cost of the juvenile justice system that deals with gang members who break the law. Gang graffiti mars the appearance of our cities and towns. Many law-abiding citizens live in fear of gang members and the havoc their illegal activities bring.

The Center for Research on Crime and Social Control study also discovered that much of gang activity is fairly recent. Law enforcement officials in over half of the cities studied said that gang activity in their town began after 1984.[5]

Easy access to guns makes today's gangs especially dangerous. In the past, gang members would fight with fists and knives. Today, many gangs have arsenals of handguns and sophisticated weapons including automatic rifles.

The human toll of gangs is tragic. In a *Newsweek* editorial, *Washington Post* columnist William Raspberry stated that in 1989 23 percent of young African-American men between the ages of twenty and twenty-nine were in prison, on parole, or on probation. Homicide was the leading cause of death for African-American males between the ages of fifteen and thirty-four. Nearly one-half of all murder victims in the United States were African American. Raspberry said, "We are losing a generation of young people, especially boys, with dire consequences for our group."[6]

As serious as the gang problem may be, it is important to remember that gang members are also human beings. They join gangs for many reasons—peer pressure, the need to belong to a group, parents who may have to work such long hours that they do not have time to be with their children. Many of the psychological needs of young gang members are the same as other young people. The gangs meet these needs.

In an interview, author Leon Bing spoke about members of the Bloods gang that she had befriended. She said, "Gang members are like families. Little kids get disciplined in gangs."[7]

Clearly, the gang problem is not a simple one. In many neighborhoods across America, gangs are a way of life. There may be gangs in your school. You may know someone who is a gang member.

It is important for young people to understand the reasons why gangs exist. It is also important to know that all gangs are alike. Street gangs have existed in America for many years. Let's take a look at how they began.

2

Gangs Are Not a New Problem

When Carlos Luis Feliciano stabbed a member of the Dragons, a rival street gang in New York, a court of the victim's friends sentenced him to be shot.

"We found a bag and put five black slips of paper in the bag and . . . wrote a 'B' (for burn) on another slip and threw it in. Then we all drew slips," said Benjamin Oliva, a member of the Seminoles, an ally of the Dragons. One of the Seminoles picked the slip with the "B" on it and had to go after Feliciano. Feliciano was killed with a sawed-off shotgun.[1]

This event occurred in 1955. Gangs may seem like a modern issue, but actually they have been a problem for many years.

Although there were street gangs in American cities in the late eighteenth century, gang activity grew in the early years of the 1800s. In the early nineteenth century, immigrants from Europe began to flock to America seeking a better life. Because most of these newcomers were poor, they were forced to live in crowded tenement (apartment) buildings, many without hot water or adequate bathrooms. Even young children worked long hours in factories for pennies a day. The opportunity for the good life that they were seeking appeared far from their grasp. Because New York City was the gateway to America, it was the first city to experience the serious problem of gang violence.

The Early Gangs of New York City

The earliest examples of organized gang violence involved white youth. Most of the early gangs of the nineteenth century were made up of Irish immigrants who lived near a park ironically named Paradise Square. Around 1826, the earliest known gang, called the Forty Thieves, was formed by a young thug named Edward Coleman. From his headquarters in a small shop that sold fruit and vegetables, Coleman sent his gang of thieves and pickpockets out to attack policemen and well-dressed gentlemen who might venture into the neighborhood.[2]

As more immigrants came to escape the famine and bad crops in Ireland, additional gangs were formed. They had names such as the Roach Guards, the Chichesters, the Shirt Tails, the Dead Rabbits, and the Plug Uglies. The Plug Uglies got their name from their huge hats stuffed with wool and leather that they wore as helmets when they went into battle. The Dead Rabbits' name came from their practice of advancing into battle

Poverty-stricken neighborhoods have long been a breeding ground for gangs. Mullen's Alley in New York's Lower East Side was home to gangs in the second half of the nineteenth century.

carrying a pole on which was jammed the body of a dead rabbit.

Soon another nearby neighborhood called the Bowery became a hub for rough gangs. The largest and most violent was the Bowery Boys who fought turf wars against the gangs of Paradise Square. Their deadly rival was the Dead Rabbits gang. The Bowery Boys were allied with other gangs of the Bowery, while the Plug Uglies, the Chichesters, and the Shirt Tails of Paradise Square fought alongside the Dead Rabbits. Gang fights might last for two or three days. During this time, the streets would be barricaded with carts and paving stones.[3]

Like today's gang members, these early gangsters were proud of their arsenals of weapons—pistols, muskets, knives, bricks, brass knuckles, clubs, ice picks, teeth, and fists. Many of these early gang members were older than gang members today. They were also smaller. Because of malnutrition, most members averaged about five feet three inches and weighed between 120 and 135 pounds. Gangs were large. Some had memberships in the hundreds.[4]

In the years following the Civil War, more violent gangs began to appear in New York City. The largest, named the Whyos, caused violence throughout the city. They were a strong force in the 1880s and early 1890s. The Whyos were known for all sorts of crimes, especially beating and murder. One member advertised that he would stab a victim for $25. For $15, he would chew off an ear, and for $100, he would commit murder.[5]

Throughout the latter part of the nineteenth century, immigrants from other parts of Europe continued to flow into American cities. Many came from the countries of Eastern Europe. Because they did not speak English, they had great difficulty adjusting to life in America. As Jewish and Italian immigrants surged into the country, youths from these ethnic groups also formed gangs.

By the beginning of the twentieth century, there was a widespread use of firearms in gang wars. One of the worst gang wars occurred in 1903 when two warring gangs, the Eastmans and the Five Pointers, waged a battle across an elevated railroad. Other gangs joined in. When the police finally succeeded in breaking up the fight, there were three dead, seven seriously wounded, and many arrests.

By this time gang life was becoming less profitable. Big Jack Zelig, who was a leader in the Eastman gang, quoted prices for injury by hire. By this time, a murder could be ordered for as little as $2 to $10.

Gangs and the Union Movement

During the early part of the twentieth century, gangs participated in movements to unionize American factories and industries.

Both workers and factory owners hired gang members to help their sides in the fight. In New York City, union leaders would hire thugs to beat and murder strikebreakers. In retaliation, the factory owners hired other toughs to guard workers who crossed picket lines. Fighting became commonplace when a strike was declared.

During this time, warring gangs still continued

In 1911, unions began hiring gang members to murder and beat strikebreakers. It was not long before factory owners began to do the same. Fighting, beating, and stabbing soon became common in labor-management disputes as seen in this drawing by Winslow Homer.

battling one another. Finally, in 1913, a new mayor, John Purroy, promised to end police corruption in New York and put down gangs. A turning point came in 1914 when an innocent bystander was shot. Purroy ordered the police to end the gang violence. Within a year, many gang leaders were in prison, and gangs appeared to be a thing of the past.[6]

By the 1920s, immigration from Europe slowed down. Better education and better jobs allowed many recent immigrants to move out of the city slums to better neighborhoods, and gang activity declined.

New York City was the largest city to experience the gang phenomenon, but it was not the only one.

Gangs in the Midwest

As far back as the 1860s, white gangs roved the streets of Chicago, much as they did in New York City. Black gangs were uncommon. Like other groups, however, as more and more African-American families migrated to Chicago, the demands of urban living created many difficulties, such as a lack of educational and employment opportunities.

In 1919, Chicago experienced a violent ethnic riot. The Chicago Commission on Race Relations reported that most of those involved in the riots were all white gangs or athletic clubs. The few black gangs who participated in the riot were mainly organized to protect their neighborhoods.

In a famous study of Chicago street gangs in 1927, criminologist Frederick M. Thrasher came to the conclusion that black street gangs made up only 7.16 percent of

White youth were most often the members of early gangs. The names of some of these young gang members from Chicago, seen with reformer and missionary Dwight Lyman Moody, tell of their vicious reputations. One is named "Butcher Kilroy." Another was called "Madden the Butcher."

the 1,313 gangs studied. The majority of gangs were still from ethnic, white immigrant communities. Gangs were especially common among the Polish, Irish, and Italians.

The 1930s did not show a noticeable increase in African-American gang activity, but by the 1940s, a few well-known African-American street gangs began to emerge. The Four Corners was a group of young African-American men who controlled the turf around the corners of 35th Street and Indiana Avenue on the Southside of Chicago. As families began to move into the Westside, black teenagers also began to form gangs, partly as protection from the white gangs that had controlled the area for years. These groups had dramatic names such as Dirty Sheiks and Wailing Shebas.

Up to the 1950s, the activities of African-American gangs mainly involved drinking, gambling, and intergroup fighting. Most of these activities were continued in the gang's neighborhood. Most of the gangs were made up of members who attended school together, and fights between these groups usually were the result of rivalry over athletics.[7]

Mexican Gangs of the Southwest

In the Southwest, Mexican immigrants were also experiencing difficult working conditions, poverty, and prejudice. Although Spanish and Mexican settlers had founded many of the cities of the Southwest, the immigrants from Mexico were forbidden to enter some parks, theaters, dance halls, and restaurants. They lived in segregated neighborhoods called *barrios*. These conditions created anger and resentment.

The earliest Mexican gang members came from the ranks of a group called *cholos*. *Cholo* was an insulting term referring to a person who was not able to fit into either the mainstream Mexican-American or the Anglo lifestyle. Sociologists say that the first generation of Mexican-Americans held onto their traditional values and did not join gangs. Children of these immigrants, however, banded together in groups, some of which had their origins in social clubs connected to the parish church. Some of the groups adopted dress codes and rituals to mark membership in the group. As the groups evolved into gangs, one of their main goals was to defend the home turf.[8]

In the late 1930s and early 1940s, some Mexican-American youth were called *pachucos*. The identifying dress of the *pachucos* was an unusual fashion called the zoot suit. The zoot suit, also called the drape shape, was distinguished by pleated, high-waisted peg trousers and a long, loose, wide-shouldered coat. The zoot suit was a fashion statement, worn by both law-abiding young men and gang members. However, the police and others in the larger community viewed the fashion with alarm because they thought the style identified gang membership. Racism played a large part in what followed.

During World War II, second generation Mexican-Americans in Los Angeles had begun to clash with the more established Anglo-American populations. They said that if they were American enough to be drafted into the armed fores, they should also be allowed to use the same parks, theaters, and clubs as the white residents. The Anglos viewed this development with alarm.

In August 1942, when the body of a young man

named José Diaz was found murdered in an abandoned gravel pit in an area near East Los Angeles, the police quickly arrested twenty-four young Mexican Americans. Although the evidence was flimsy, twelve were found guilty of murder and five of assault. They were set free two years later when their convictions were overturned by the district court of appeals because the evidence against them was considered so weak. Unfortunately, eight of the young men had served close to two years in San Quentin prison.

A short time after the incident, *pachucos* wearing zoot suits and teenage Anglos began starting fights in downtown Los Angeles. The police began arresting young men who looked like *pachucos*, saying they were gang members. Local newspapers used headlines like "Guerilla Gang Warfare" and "Juvenile Hoodlums" to report the incident, fanning the public's emotions.

On Thursday, June 3, 1943, a gang of zoot-suiters attacked eleven sailors in downtown Los Angeles. The next night, 200 sailors invaded the *barrios* on the east side of the city. Four youths were beaten. A few nights later, eight teenagers were beaten in another *barrio*. The following night, a mob of several thousand servicemen and civilians swarmed over downtown Los Angeles dragging anyone dressed like a *pachuco* into the streets, beating him mercilessly. Many were not members of any gang.[9]

Gangs of the 1950s, 1960s, 1970s

During World War II, many African Americans and Puerto Ricans moved to northern and western cities to

A group of Mexican-American men leave jail for a court appearance following their arrests for wearing zoot suits, a popular style in the 1940s that was sometimes associated with gang affiliation. Those who adopted the style were called *pachucos*. Some were in gangs. Others were not.

work in the war efforts. In New York City, many moved into Italian, Jewish, and Irish neighborhoods. The older residents viewed the newcomers with hostility. Outbreaks of violence were common, and some of the young people banded together into gangs to defend their neighborhoods.

It wasn't long before some of the gangs went out looking for trouble. Fighting gangs or cliques were identified by the way they walked. They would rhythmically swagger with each step. In neighborhoods of the Lower East Side, youths would wear leather jackets with nickel stars on the shoulders. The jackets might be made to order with special colors and names of the club or perhaps a baseball team on the back.[10]

The 1950s also saw the beginnings of the powerful Vice Lord Nation, a federation of street-corner cliques or gangs in Chicago. The Vice Lords probably originated in the Illinois State Training School for Boys in St. Charles, Illinois, also called "Charleytown." In the fall of 1958, several young men recently released from the prison brought the gang to the Lawndale area of Chicago, long a breeding ground for Jewish, African-American, and Polish gangs. The Vice Lord Nation was made up of African-American youth. The principal rival of the Vice Lords was a gang called the Cobras. This gang started in the Maxwell Street open market area of Chicago's west side.[11]

In the 1950s, many gang members turned to marijuana and heroin to escape the problems of their lives. As drug use began to increase, authorities noticed that gang activity decreased. Because drug abuse was considered a problem of the ghetto, many authorities did not take it seriously.[12]

In the mid-1960s, many of the ghettos of American cities were torn by rioting and rebellion. In Newark (New Jersey), Detroit, Chicago, the Watts district of Los Angeles, Washington, D.C., and other cities, people took to the streets, setting fires, looting shops, and fighting the police. In the aftermath of the riots, groups such as the Black Muslims, the Black Panthers, and the Young Lords, a Puerto Rican group in East Harlem, formed to stop police brutality and to force the government to improve services to the people of the ghetto. For a while, many viewed these groups as role models because they became involved in their communities.[13]

By the 1970s, gang warfare was again making headlines. In 1973, reporter Martin Tolchin wrote a four-part series of articles about the poverty and gangs in the South Bronx for the *New York Times*. The incidents he described included an invasion of a bus by a gang who held the driver at gunpoint while passengers' wallets were stolen and a young girl was beaten with chains.[14]

By the mid 1970s, gang members came from many different ethnic groups. Although Latinos made up one third of the gangs in New York City, there were also Filipino, Japanese, newly immigrated Hong Kong Chinese as well as African-American and white gangs. At this time, in other large American cities the majority of gang members were between the ages of ten and twenty-one, although in Chicago and Philadelphia a number were as young as eight. In large cities, gangs were operating within many junior and senior high schools.[15]

The 1970s also brought an increasing use of firearms, many of which were similar to high-quality police weapons.

Since the 1970s, gangs have continued to be a serious problem in most cities and towns in America. Gangs have even migrated to rural areas, far from large urban centers.

Clearly, gangs have been a problem for over 150 years. The next chapter will look at the way gangs are different from other groups.

3

What Is a Gang?

Unlike normal social groups of young people, youth gangs or street gangs are groups that are often motivated by violence and illegal activities that range from defacing property and fighting to drug- and weapon-trafficking. A gang can be very large with subdivisions determined by age. Some gangs are very small. Sometimes smaller gangs, called posses, sets, or cliques, unite under the umbrella of a larger gang, such as the Crips or the Bloods in southern California.

Let's look at the way some experts define gangs. One definition states that gangs must meet three criteria: Members must recognize themselves as a distinct group; the community must recognize the gang as a group; and the gang must involve itself in enough illegal activities to get a consistent negative response from the community and from law enforcement.[1]

Gang Prevention Through Targeted Outreach, prepared by a department of the U.S. Department of Justice and published by the Boys and Girls Clubs of America, classifies gangs into territorial gangs, organized gangs, and scavenger groups.

Territorial gangs, also known as turf or hood gangs, work to control a geographic area, which might be a block, a neighborhood, or a building. A school located in the neighborhood might also be considered a part of the gang's turf.

Organized, instrumental, or corporate gangs have a strict organization that is almost military. There is a definite leader, a warlord, armskeeper, treasurer, enforcers, and foot soldiers. This structure is necessary to smoothly run illegal activities, such as drug dealing where large sums of money are involved.

Members of scavenger gangs are attracted to the group because it gives them a sense of belonging. They may not have strictly defined leadership, organization, and turf, but they usually do agree upon common behavior.[2]

How Gangs Evolve

Gangs usually develop from groups of troublemaking young people who may share a common neighborhood, school, or interest. Their friendship and associations lead to illegal acts such as painting graffiti, theft, and other minor crimes.

In *People and Folks, Gangs, Crime and the Underclass in a Rustbelt City*, author James M. Hagedorn describes the origins of gangs in Milwaukee, where gangs became a

A territorial gang will often mark its neighborhood or turf with graffiti. Crossing out a rival gang's graffiti is considered an act of war.

serious problem in the 1980s. Of nineteen gangs in Milwaukee in 1988, ten grew out of neighborhood groups, three had their origins as dancing groups, four came from Chicago, and two were made up of girls associated with male gangs.[3]

The Milwaukee gangs follow a pattern that sets them apart from other organized groups of young people. Some of these traits are initiation rituals, dislike of school, accumulation of weapons, and extremely strong attachment and loyalty to one another.[4]

Some larger gangs in Milwaukee are organized into age groupings such as "pee wees," ages 8–11; "juniors," 12–15; main group or "seniors," 16–19; "ancients," "veterans," or "old gangsters," 20 and up. "Wannabees" are young people who hang around the fringes of the gang.[5]

Membership in a gang may span many ages from children to adults. Youngsters can begin to form gang allegiances in the early years of elementary school. In some cases, babies and toddlers whose parents are gang members are almost certain to be raised into a gang lifestyle. Many adults keep their gang affiliations, too.

Since World War II, authorities have noticed that some gang members are much younger than those of the past. Today, some gangs recruit boys and girls who are still in elementary school. Still, juveniles under eighteen are a minority of gang membership. In Los Angeles County, juveniles made up only 20 percent of total gang membership.[6]

According to statistics gathered by the Los Angeles County District Attorney's office, the youngest gang members in that jurisdiction were eight years old. The oldest members were in their sixties. However, the peak ages for gang activity were between the ages of mid-to-late teens and early twenties. Some members stay active through their twenties and thirties.

Serious gang affiliation can begin as early as second grade. However, for most young people, gang membership begins in the pre-teen years or later. The average age of shooters in gang-related homicides is around twenty.[7]

Traditionally, most gang members have been male, but gangs also attract women. In the past, most women in gangs were in auxiliaries or branches of male gangs. Some gangs are made up of both males and females. There are also independent female gangs similar to male gangs.

All ethnic groups have gangs; however, gangs may vary from one ethnic group to another. Some gangs cut across ethnic and racial lines. An ethnic gang group is a group that defines itself by a common culture, heritage, or country of origin of its members. There are several major ethnic street gangs in the United States.

Mexican-American Gangs of the Southwest

Mexican-American gangs have existed in the Southwest since the early part of the twentieth century. Some of these gangs have membership that spans generations.

"The Hispanic gangs got their start in the steamy barrios of East L.A. where they fought each other for dominion over school yards and street corners . . . it was the *cholo* homeboy who first walked the walk and talked the talk. It was the Mexican-American *pachuco* who initiated the emblematic tattoos, the signing with hands, the

CRITERIA FOR DEFINING GANGS

Criteria Used	Large Cities*	Smaller Cities*
Use of Symbols	93%	100%
Violent Behavior	81%	84%
Group Organization	81%	88%
Territory	74%	88%
Leadership	59%	48%
Recurrent Interaction	56%	60%

* Of the cities surveyed, 70 (89%) of the large cities and 25 (58%) of the smaller cities indicated the criteria used to define gangs.

Source: 1992 NIJ Gang Survey

writing of legends on walls," writes author Leon Bing in *Do or Die*, a book about African-American gangs in Los Angeles.[8]

Mexican-American gang members, sometimes called *cholos*, often could be identified by what they wore— khaki pants, white tee shirts, and plain Pendelton jackets. Girl gang members, called *cholas*, often wore exaggerated makeup and dyed their hair blond or red-blond.

Recently, this style of dress has changed. Gang members still might wear khaki pants. They also favor black pants and black jackets. Black L.A. Raiders football team caps are also popular. Girls often dress in the same manner as boys.

In recent years, as immigration from Mexico and Central America has surged, Latino gangs have spread beyond the Southwest. Today, there are such gangs in cities of the Midwest and East. Youths from Central America have also banded together in gangs such as the Salvatruches, a Salvadoran gang active in Los Angeles.

Puerto Rican Gangs of New York City

In the late 1940s and 1950s, there was a flood of immigration from Puerto Rico, a territory of the United States. Many of these immigrants settled in New York City. Some of the children of these immigrants formed gangs for self-defense and to get a feeling of solidarity. The gangs, also called *gangas* or *pandillas*, usually are territorial. Some of the gangs are mixed racially; others are all Puerto Rican.[9]

The members identify one another by their hats or

jackets, which often have an emblem or other insignia. Girls are organized into a girls' branch or auxiliary. The gang might have members ranging from boys and girls as young as ten or eleven to young adults.[10]

Jamaican and Dominican gangs are also active in New York City. Many of these gangs are involved in drug distribution.

African-American Gangs

African-American gang members are often associated with Los Angeles gangs called the Crips or the Bloods, or the Chicago gangs, called the Vice Lords or the Folk Nation. These groups are territorial and in some cases are organized and tightly structured. Some are involved in the distribution of drugs.

Paul Jones, a crisis intervention supervisor with the Community Youth Gang Services in South Central Los Angeles says that the Crips began sometime in the early 1970s as a group from Washington Fundamental School. They took the color of that school—blue—as their trademark. Crips sometimes wear blue striped running shoes and shoelaces, blue jackets, and blue bandannas. Some people believe the Crips got their name because of their practice of shooting victims in the kneecaps, crippling them. The Bloods began in Compton, a suburb of Los Angeles. Their color is red.[11]

The Crips and the Bloods are organized into smaller neighborhood groups called sets. Playboy Gangster Crips, the 8 Tray Gangster Crips, and the Five Deuce Broadways are examples of Crip sets. The Bounty Hunters and the Piru Bloods are examples of sets that identify with the Bloods gang. Crips and Bloods are bitter enemies. Sets within the gangs also feud with one another over turf.

Gang colors are important trademarks of the gang. People have been shot for wearing the wrong colors in the wrong neighborhood. Like all styles, however, gang fashions change. Now, gang members do not always look like they did in the past. Some may even wear suits, says Paul Jones.

The African-American gangs of Chicago dress in a manner that is very different from the Crips and the Bloods. The Black Gangster Discipline Nation adopts the colors black and blue and tilt their hats toward the right. The Vice Lord gang wears red and black. Members wear their earrings in the left ear and tilt their hats to the left.[12]

Chinese, Cambodian, and Vietnamese Gangs

Chinese gangs are more secretive than African-American or Hispanic gangs. They are organizational gangs whose specialty is extortion and robbery in Asian communities. (Extortion is demanding money for protection with the threat of violence if refused.)

In New York City, Chinese gangs began to spring up in the 1960s and 1970s. Members dress in black and may have their chests and arms tattooed with serpents, dragons, and eagles. Some of the members are as young as thirteen. In nearby Queens, two rival gangs are the Green Tigers and the White Tigers. Chinese gangs are tightly organized under a leader called the *dai lo*. The

GANG MEMBERS IN 1991 BY ETHNICITY

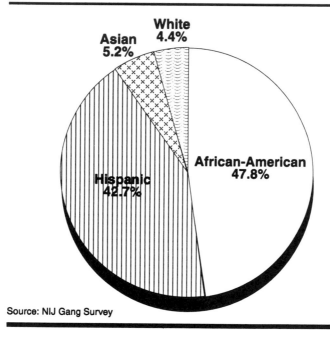

Source: NIJ Gang Survey

The National Institute of Justice studied the ethnicity of gang membership in sixteen cities. Between 1990 and 1991 African-American gang members increased by 13 percent. Latino gang members increased by 18 percent. There were fewer overall numbers of white and Asian gang members, but their numbers were found to be increasing by a higher percent. In cities where data were available, the number of Asian gang members increased by 66 percent, and the number of white gang members by 55 percent.

junior members are expected to follow instructions even if they are ordered to commit a murder.[13]

Crime among Vietnamese and Cambodian youth is also on the rise. These groups came to the United States as immigrants after the Vietnam War. Household robberies in Orange County, California, where many Vietnamese immigrants live are a serious problem.

Cambodian gangs are active in Long Beach, California, and in Lowell, Massachusetts. Both communities have large groups of Cambodian immigrants. In August 1991, rivalry between the Tiny Rascals and the Thunder Group, two Cambodian gangs in Lowell, erupted into violence when five boys, including a twelve-year-old, were shot while they were playing basketball in an elementary school yard. The shooting was believed to be related to an early attack on a fifteen-year-old member of the Tiny Rascals.[14] In Long Beach, Cambodian gangs battle with Mexican-American gangs over turf.

"At school, the Mexicans looked down upon us and hurt us," recalls Mad Dog, twenty-nine, a "retired" homeboy whose mother was a Phnom Phen university professor. "We saw that American people had groups, white with white, black with black. We decided to become more famous. If they could steal cars and do drive-by shoots, so could we."[15]

White gangs

Early gangs in the United States were made up of poor white young people. Today, whites still join gangs.

Skinheads are young people who adopt the fashion of closely shaving their heads. They began to appear in the United States in the 1980s. It is estimated that there are approximately 3,000 to 4,000 skinheads in the United States. They are usually white males between the ages of fourteen and twenty-four. Skinheads often tattoo their bodies with Nazi symbols such as swastikas and lightning bolts. They wear steel-toed Doc Marten boots, which they may use to kick with in fights. They also wear blue or black denim pants or six-pocket fatigues and black or green flight jackets.[16] According to the National Council of Churches, in the mid-1980s skinheads were responsible for 121 known murders, 302 assaults, and 301 cross burnings. Most of the crimes were against minorities.

The White Aryan Resistance (W.A.R.) is an adult hate group founded by racist Tom Metzger. It has focused on recruitment of young skinheads for one of the organization's branches, the W.A.R. Skins, probably the single largest group of skinheads. In 1989, this group numbered approximately 1,400 members.[17]

Groups of white youth also band together to commit illegal acts such as stealing, robberies, defacing public or private property, muggings, or rape. Some are ethnic gangs—Irish or Armenian, for example. Others, like the Spur Posse, a clique of white high school athletes in Lakewood, California, are suburban cliques that show gang-like behavior. The Spur Posse took turns having sex with girls, keeping score and bragging about it to their friends. One eleven-year-old girl was raped by a young man who came through a bedroom window while she was sleeping at a friend's house.[18] "I have friends who were beaten up and raped by them," said one

Gang graffiti defaces both public and private property. Removing graffiti takes time and money and is an ongoing process in many neighborhoods where gangs and taggers are active. Sometimes those found guilty of minor offenses are sentenced to graffiti removal as a requirement of probation.

sixteen-year-old girl. "If a girl would not sleep with them, they would beat her up."[19]

Tagging Posses, Crews, or Cliques

Taggers, people who mark territory with graffiti, also show some gang-like behavior. They use spray paint or markers to write their names on buildings, walls, freeway overpasses, buses, and on any other space they can find. Members in a tagging posse, crew, or clique are not all from the same neighborhood or race, and organization is fairly loose. Some taggers will fight to keep other groups from crossing out or defacing their graffiti. Taggers often wear baggy clothes to conceal spray cans. Law enforcement agencies consider tagging groups as gangs. The cost of their vandalism is huge. The National Graffiti Information Network estimates that it costs $4.5 billion dollars annually to remove graffiti. Although taggers are not usually violent, some of the tagging posses carry weapons to protect themselves. Taggers have been killed in fights with rivals.[20]

Suburban Gangs

Gangs are much more widespread than they were in the past when they were primarily a problem in large cities.

In the late 1980s, law enforcement officials in Massachusetts towns such as Brockton and Milton began to notice that youth gangs from Boston were taking field trips to the suburbs to socialize. They were drawn by the malls and movie theaters. They also visited former members whose parents had moved out of Boston to get their children out of the gang environment. Rather than

GANG CRIME PROBLEMS BY SITE, 1992

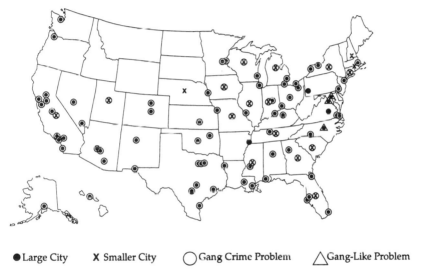

● Large City   X Smaller City   ○ Gang Crime Problem   △ Gang-Like Problem

Source: NIJ Gang Survey

Ninety-one percent of large city police departments reported the presence within their jurisdictions of criminally involved groups with youths as members that they labeled as "gangs." Three other cities reported groups that were gang-like but they were called crews, posses or drug organizations.

leaving the gang, some of these transplanted gang members brought their criminal habits with them. In 1991, Brockton had its first gang-related shooting and six gang-related murders.[21]

Whatever their origins, it is clear that gangs are a growing problem. In November 1991, it was estimated that New York had about 50 gangs with 5,000 members; Chicago had 125 gangs with 12,500 members; Dallas had 225 gangs; Los Angeles had more than 900 gangs with about 100,000 members; and Miami reported a 1,000 percent increase in gangs and gang membership between 1986 and 1991.[22]

4

Girls and Gangs

Not much is known about the roles of females in gangs and the reasons why they join. Some gangs are made up of both males and females. Some females are part of auxiliary gangs associated with an all-male gang. Girlfriends or sweethearts of male gang members may hang out with the gang without actually joining. There is also a new phenomenon of all-girl gangs who run together and commit violent and illegal acts, much in the same way as males.

Although there are many fewer females than males in gangs, they have long been involved in gang life. As far back as the early Irish gangs in New York City, girls have played a part in gang violence. Some of the early street gangs even had girl leaders. The Forty Little Thieves, a pack of young boys and girls associated with the Forty Thieves gang, was led by a young girl named Wild

Maggie Carson. Although Wild Maggie lived up to her name as a fighter, she left the gang life at the age of twelve when she was converted to religion.[1]

Usually, the girls belonged to female gangs affiliated with male gangs. Some of the names of these nineteenth-century girl gangs were the Lady Gophers, the Lady Locusts, the Lady Flashers, and the Lady Truck Drivers Association. Battle Annie, the leader of the Lady Gophers' was notorious. She held classes to train the women of her gang in combat.[2]

When criminologist Frederick Thrasher studied the gangs of Chicago in 1927, he could locate only five or six all-female gangs. Four of these were social clubs, one was organized around baseball and one around stealing. Some of the clubs located by Thrasher had names like the Tulips, the Lone Star Club, the Under-the-L gang, and the Night Riders. Most of the gangs were made up of white females. Thrasher came to the opinion that at that time there were fewer girls than boys in the Chicago gangs because girls had more family supervision and were more influenced by tradition and custom than were the boys.[3]

In 1949, when researcher William Bernard studied gangs in New York City, he discovered a number of young women in the gangs he observed. Because they could not be searched by male police officers, the girls often carried weapons for the boys. They also provided alibis, acted as spies and lures, and provided sex for the male members. When they fought the members of rival girl gangs, they were known to throw a mixture of lye and soda in the faces of their enemies.

Leadership of these girls' gangs usually included a

president, a prime minister, or a war counselor. In the 1950s and 1960s the Dagger Debs, a Puerto Rican gang in New York City, was affiliated with a male gang called the Daggers. The girls wore men's shirts, dungarees, boots with pointed toes, and red bandannas. Their club-house was an abandoned apartment. The girls were involved in mugging, fighting, shoplifting, and providing sex for male gang members.[4]

In the Deaconettes, an African-American girls' gang in Chicago in the 1940s, members would sometimes be involved in rumbles or fights with other female gangs. By the 1960s, such female gangs had almost disappeared. Girls had become a part of the criminal acts of male gangs, serving as lookouts, shoplifters, and concealers of weapons and illegal goods.[5]

In 1964, author Kitty Hanson described a gang fight in her book *Rebels in the Street, the Story of New York's Girl Gangs:*

> Hanky was a fighter, but no match for the fury that jerked her off the park bench, gouged sharp nails the length of one cheek, punched in the stomach and then pounded her into unconsciousness. Truelove leaped upon the prostrate girl, kicking and stomping and kicking until her boots were bloody.[6]

In a study done in 1974, it was discovered that half of the New York gangs had female branches, but girls only made up 6 percent of the total gang membership of the city at that time. In Chicago, there were 4,400 gang-related arrests, but only 400 were of females.[7]

In 1974, John Quicker, a California sociologist studied girl gangs in the barrios of East Los Angeles. Most of the girls belonged to female branches of male gangs, although some belonged to gangs that included members of both sexes. The initiation rites he described have not changed much in Hispanic gangs today.

In order to join a gang, a girl would have to express interest and prove her bravery. There were two forms of initiation—jumping in and a fair fight. If a girl were jumped in, she would have to defend herself from being beaten by older girls in the gang for at least ten seconds. She might also have a "fair fight" with an established gang member. A few girls were "walked in" without an initiation. To leave the gang, she would have to be "jumped out" or beaten up by members. Some girls might leave without fighting if they married or got a job. The gang required strict loyalty, and the girls referred to one another as "home girl" or "sister."[8]

In some Latino gangs, girls look up to an older woman, or *veterana*, in her twenties or thirties who gives advice and counsel on gang, personal, and romantic matters. Although a girl is supposed to choose her boyfriend from the affiliated male gang and be faithful to him while they are going together, she might also be able to have a boyfriend who is not in a gang. Associating with a male from a rival gang, however, is not tolerated.

The girls fight members of rival female gangs whom they insult by calling them "ho's" (whores) or "glue-sniffers." Like boys, they will invade an enemy territory to paint their *placas*, or gang names, which throws a challenge to the rivals. Although the boys fight with guns, the girls commonly use knives or their fists in combat. Although these girls are tough, they follow a traditional

GANG-RELATED CRIME BY TYPE AS PERCENT OF TOTAL RECORDED BY GENDER

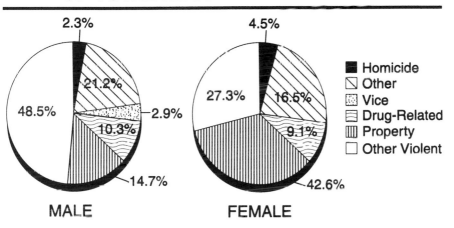

Note: No gang-related crime was reported in the Vice category for females.

Source: NIJ Gang Survey

Although there are fewer females in gangs, they are involved in very violent crimes. Proportionally, almost twice as many female gang-related crimes were homicides (4.5 percent for females and 2.3 percent for males). Violent offenses not resulting in homicide were proportionally much more common for male gang offenders, while property crimes were more common for female offenders.

submissive role when they are with their gang boyfriends.[9]

In mixed-sex gangs, which have become more common since the 1970s, girls fight along with the boys. The girls may join without initiation fights. They gain their reputation by fighting in gang wars, by defending the gang's name at school or on the street, and by fighting girls from rival gangs. The girls might also assist the gang by acting as spies or decoys or by luring rival gang members into a situation where they could be ambushed.[10]

Gangs are still primarily a male activity. Of the nineteen gangs in Milwaukee, only three included females. The 2-7 Syndicates and the V-L Queens were girl affiliates of male gangs. The Sheiks, a dance-based gang, had a male auxiliary called the "Boy Sheiks."[11]

What Leads Girls to Join Gangs?

Like males, they are often poor. Many attend segregated schools where their achievement is low. Their lives may appear to have little hope. For some, the gang is the way of life in their neighborhood. There may be a history of gang membership in their families. As with boys, girls join gangs because they give a sense of family and provide excitement through partying and illegal activities.

LT, a young teenage girl quoted in *Letters from a Teenage Jail*, edited by Joseph Bauer, described the life of a chola, or gang girl, in a barrio, or neighborhood, of southern California:

> I've been a Gang Banger for 3 years and in and out
> of jail since the age of 14. I used to party every day,
> all night long with my homies. Not giving a care

46

on how my family felt or what time I got home eather.[sic] I'd come home just to sleep, eat, and dress and steal money to support my drug habits. It's pretty hard staying in house where your own family don't trust you any more. So, it came to a point where I loved my homies and mi varrio more than my own flesh and blood.[12]

Today, many girls associated with gangs follow a similar path to that followed by girls of earlier generations. Running with the gang means providing sexual favors to gang members, fighting girls from other gangs, and engaging in illegal activities such as shoplifting. Girls may also be involved in drive-by shootings and other more serious crimes. The behavior of these groups can be very violent, frequently leading to injury and arrest. Often, these girls are very nonchalant when they are arrested and questioned for their offenses. A female gang member in Detroit even bragged to researchers about shooting an Uzi to get rid of some unwanted party guests.[13]

In 1991 in New York City, posses or groups of young people, both boys and girls, prowled the streets, attacking and robbing innocent victims. These attacks were called "wilings" or "wildings." In one instance, a thirteen-year-old girl whose Swahili name meant Gift from God was arrested for participating in an all-girl group attack on a thirteen-year-old Latino girl in a Harlem subway. The Latino girl was stomped and sexually assaulted. During questioning, Gift from God—who had a semicircular scar on her cheek from a bite wound and a line of stitches where a razor had sliced her ear in half—was asked if the local boys liked girls who were hard. She replied, "If you hard you don't need boys."

Another crew or posse of twelve- and thirteen-year-old girls was rounded up and arrested at their school for stomping a pregnant woman on the subway. The girls joked and laughed while they were being taken to the headquarters of the Transit Police. As they stepped from the police van, they waved at a group of boys across the street and giggled.[14]

Gangs and Teenage Pregnancy

Whether a girl is in a gang or is a girlfriend of a gang member, her association with gang life does not usually foster a good self-image. In spite of their tough exteriors, girls are influenced by the low regard given them by boys in the gang. Girls are referred to as "ho's" or "OPP" (Other People's Property). "Girls are considered trash, somebody there to serve the boys. Black gangs, Latino gangs—I don't see much difference on this. The same treatment is being afforded girls in Asian gangs," said Bert Davila, director of gang operations for the Los Angeles County Probation Department.[15]

Lack of self-esteem and future goals leads these girls to become sexually active at a very young age. Many become mothers while still in their early teens. A *Los Angeles Times* study on birth rates among young teens noted a rise in childbearing among gang members who talked about wanting to leave something behind in case they die young.[16]

A girl who bears a child while she is still a child herself faces many difficulties. These problems are even more severe when the young mother is involved with a gang member. While these young mothers often say they want to make a baby for their homeboy, more often than not, gang members make unreliable fathers. Hard-core gang members are less likely to become live-in fathers. Many end up in prison. Others are too immature to face the responsibilities of parenthood, leaving the young women to fend for themselves and their children.

One boy with a street name of "Mite" is typical. Although he is the father of a one-year-old son, he does not live with the child's mother, and he does not support the child financially. He views his son as something to play with. He sometimes dresses the child in gang colors, and he wanted to give the baby a tattoo.[17]

According to statistics of the Los Angeles County District Attorney's Office, most female gang members face a hopeless future. Ninety-four percent of gang girls will have children, and 84 percent will raise them without a partner or spouse. Most will depend on welfare. As the girls leave adolescence, most gradually leave the gang. Their reasons include drug addiction, prison, marriage or relationship with a man, or having children. Most are caught in an endless cycle of poverty and welfare.[18]

5

The Lure of the Gangs

No one knows for sure why young people join gangs, but most experts agree that there are many causes. Sociologists and social workers believe that poverty, lack of opportunity, and racism play a large role in the development of gangs. Other causes are social problems such as broken homes and the breakdown of family values. Some say that gangs are glamorized in the media. The excitement of participating in illegal and criminal activity draws some young people to gang activity. Gangs provide other members with a social life. Some join gangs for security and protection.

Poverty, Lack of Opportunity, and Racism

Although many young people grow up in poor and run-down neighborhoods without joining a gang, others see gangs as a way to cope with the frustrations of living in

Many young people still live in neighborhoods with boarded up businesses, defaced buildings and few recreational facilities. These conditions encourage gang activities.

Many children, especially those with unsupervised and unstructured discretionary time, are in danger of joining gangs. These young people at the Boys and Girls Clubs, pictured with actor and former Club member Denzel Washington, have an advantage. Boys and Girls Clubs, known as "the Positive Place for Kids," provide young people with facility-based and professionally-staffed activities on a daily basis.

limiting conditions. Unfortunately, there are still many people living in poverty throughout the United States. Many are new immigrants from Latin America and Asia. Others are African Americans, whites, and Latinos whose ancestors have lived here for many generations. Often these people live in clusters in the older, rundown sections of large cities. Like the slums of the nineteenth century, these blighted neighborhoods are often breeding grounds for gang activity. Children who live in these neighborhoods may believe that their future is without hope. Being in a gang brings them acceptance and a sense of power.

"Poverty plays a tremendous part in people becoming involved in gangs," said Paul Jones of the Community Youth Gang Services agency in Los Angeles. "There's a tremendous amount of camaraderie, unity and actual love that one receives from being in a gang. If I'm a human being wanting and seeking power and recognition, it stands to reason that I'll pull in with people with like feelings to mine. This happens over and over. Those who feel powerless get their power through the gang."

In many poor families, the parents must struggle to make ends meet. Some work at more than one job, leaving their children unsupervised. Some of these young people are drawn into a gang because it provides the structure that they have not found at home. "It's security—so you're in a fight. You're not out there by yourself. It's like a family environment," said a Boston youth worker.[1]

Many people believe that there is a growing underclass in America that does not have the same mobility as the rest of the country. During the 1980s in Milwaukee, there were twice as many African-American workers in factory and low-paying service jobs than in management or professional occupations. As the decade progressed, more and more of these factory jobs were lost across America, creating a high level of unemployment.

In the past, young people often left the gangs as they entered the workplace. Today, their prospects of getting a good job are bleak. Many are unemployed or work at low-level jobs. Some go on to receive welfare. Others make money in illegal ways, such as dealing drugs.[2]

Racism also plays a role in creating gangs in under-privileged communities. (Racism is suspicion, intolerance or hatred of a person because of his or her race or ethnic background.) People from minority groups often believe that they receive poor treatment from police and other people in positions of authority. Often, schools in minority neighborhoods have fewer resources than those in suburban neighborhoods. They may also be over-crowded. Young people in these inner-city schools have complained that they are not encouraged to take difficult courses. Many drop out by high school. Most dropouts do not have the skills to find a good job.

Another way racism has affected minorities is through the media—television and movies. Often minorities are portrayed in a negative way, leading to stereotypes. (Stereotypes are a set of traits or characteristics attributed to an entire group of people.) In the past, African Americans and Latinos were often depicted as lazy. Stereotypes are damaging because they give many people a low self-image. Young people who have low self-esteem are particularly susceptible to the lure of

Often, youth in poor neighborhoods go to schools that have fewer facilities than are found in suburban schools. High fences are built to protect both students and the facilities. They also keep gang members and drug dealers from entering the school grounds.

gangs. They need the support of the gang to give them a feeling of worth. The yearning for respect can be seen in the names of some of the gangs. In New York City in the 1950s, gangs had names like Imperial Counts, Viceroys, Enchanters, and Noble Englishmen. Statistics from the Los Angeles County Sheriff's Department show that the many gangs come from minority communities where poverty and lack of opportunity present serious problems. As of April 15, 1993, the gangs in Los Angeles County broke down in this pattern:

Gang Types	Number of gangs
Crips (African American)	225 sets
Bloods (African American)	84 sets
Hispanic	560 separate gangs
Asian	81 separate gangs
White	20 separate gangs
Taggers	842 posses[3]

A similar pattern is found in New York City where 50 percent of the gang members are Puerto Rican and 35 percent are African American. Many come from the poorest areas of the Bronx and Brooklyn.[4]

"Gangs flourish when there's a lack of social recreation, decent education or employment," wrote author Luis Rodriguez. "Today, many young people will never know what it is to work. They can only satisfy their needs through collective strength—against the police, who hold the power of life and death, against poverty, against idleness, against their impotence in society."[5]

Father Gregory J. Boyle, a Jesuit priest who worked with young gang members in East Los Angeles, believes that the feeling of worthlessness among poor young people leads them to dangerous risk-taking through gang activities.[6]

However, it is also important to remember that most youth who are immigrants, members of a minority community, or live in a rundown neighborhood never join a gang. Poverty and lack of opportunity are not the only causes for gang involvement.

Recent Immigrants as Gang Members

During the past twenty years, many immigrants have come to the United States to escape war and destruction or political problems in their native countries. Others have come for economic reasons. They come to the United States to escape poverty and build a better life for their families. Some immigrant youth have a problem in achieving a sense of identity in their new country. They must struggle with getting along in two cultures, that of their families and that of their adopted country. Adjusting to a new language, a new culture, and new values is difficult for many teens.

Immigrant parents may not understand American customs such as American-style dating, music, and clothing. When people try to balance the values of their native culture with those of their new country, they may feel frustrated and confused. For some, joining a gang appears a way to cope with their frustrations.

Adding to the problem, many young people witnessed death and destruction in their countries before moving to the United States. While some are able to come to terms with their past, others are drawn to violent behavior. Such is the case with members of gangs made up of Cambodian youth who came to the United States to flee the revolution in the country of their birth. Social workers say that many of these youths have witnessed the killing or starvation of relatives while they were growing up in overcrowded refugee camps along the border between Cambodia and Thailand.

"They dodged bombs and saw their relatives killed," said one researcher. In California, some Cambodian gang members bring sophisticated weapons such as AK-47s to a fight.[7]

Other Reasons for Joining a Gang

"The child without a secure family life is forced either into aggression and delinquency or into apathy and despair," wrote Kenneth B. Clark in his book, *Dark Ghetto*.[8] Although Clark was writing about African-American ghetto life, his words could today take a broader meaning as many teenagers from all ethnic groups are growing up in families that are not meeting a young person's needs for love, security, and guidance. The gang becomes a substitute family.

Peer pressure is another reason why some young people join a gang. If a young person's friends are in a gang, it may be hard not to join. Luis Rodriguez's son Ramiro joined a gang when he was fifteen. He had moved to Chicago to live with his father after he began to fail in school in Los Angeles. Adjusting to life in a new school and learning to live with his father's new family was not easy. At seventeen, he was a senior in high school and had an after-school job. Although his life was on track, he still belonged to the gang for the friendship and camaraderie. "I've put my heart into the gang I'm in now," he says. "That's why I haven't got out. They're like my brothers."[9]

"Kids seek out peers like themselves," said Sergeant Wes McBride of the Los Angeles Sheriff's Department. Some kids ask to join, perhaps motivated by a desire for acceptance.

Family traditions also lead some to join a gang, especially in neighborhoods where there are generational gangs—groups that might include uncles, grandfathers, fathers, and cousins. In these families, joining a gang is looked upon with pride.

Some neighborhoods accept the gang as a form of protection because gang members will act as vigilantes to defend the neighborhood. In one New York neighborhood studied by author Martin Sanchez Jankowski, gang members provided an escort service for the elderly.[10]

In some rough neighborhoods, kids join gangs for protection. The gang is a place to belong. It may promote parties and dances. It can be a source for drugs, alcohol, and girls. Illegal activities such as drug dealing are also a source for making money. A young gang member bragged to a Detroit researcher about his illegal activities:

> My momma talk about how proud she is of me making doughski. She used to dog me and say I wasn't s—, but now she's proud.[11]

Low performance in school makes a young person vulnerable to gang recruitment. In Chinese gangs, for example, older members seek out youths who are school dropouts or who are doing poorly in school.[12]

When researchers questioned about 200 male gang members and 400 nongang youths from gang neighborhoods in Los Angeles, Chicago, and San Diego, they found that those who didn't join a gang shared similar family traits, age, and race with those who did join a gang. The gang members, however, were more likely to be school dropouts.[13]

Movies and television coverage of gangs also plays a role in making gangs attractive and fashionable for some kids. "When young people keep hearing about gangs, they're going to gravitate toward them," says Paul Jones of the Community Youth Gang Services in Los Angeles.

6

Gang Life

When one thinks about gangs, the picture of brutal fights, drive-by shootings, and other illegal activity most often comes to mind. Although violence is a part of gang life, much of the activity of the gang involves hanging out, socializing, and partying to relieve the boredom that comes from a lack of meaningful work, recreation, or school activity. Gangs today are not too different from gangs of the past. Jacob Riis, a nineteenth-century reformer, wrote about gang life on New York's Lower East Side:

> They have their "club rooms" where they meet, generally in a tenement, sometimes under a pier or a dump, to carouse, play cards, and plan their raids; their "fences," who dispose of stolen property.[1]

Life in today's gangs involves recruitment of new

Gangs have always enjoyed socializing or "hanging out" together. Part of the socialization is wearing a similar style of clothing. The Short Street gang, active in the New York waterfront area in the 19th century, would pirate cargo ships and murder watchmen and passers-by. Here they are seen in their hang-out, under the pier at the foot of Jackson Street, now Corlears Hook Park.

members, initiation into the gang, common unifying behavior such as graffiti, loyalty to turf or 'hood, dress, tattoos, codes of conduct, language and hand signs, designation of leadership, and ultimately a ritual for leaving the gang.[2]

Joining the Gang

To maintain a strong image and presence, a gang must recruit new members to its ranks. "Wannabees," youth who adopt the styles and language of a gang to indicate their interest in joining, are likely candidates. Gangs also frighten young people into joining by threatening them or their family's safety. Some young people who are not really drawn to the gang may join for survival in a gang-controlled neighborhood.

The actual joining of the gang may involve being beaten up or participation in an illegal activity to prove one's toughness and value to the gang.[3]

Proving trustworthiness and loyalty are also important. "You have to prove yourself that you're down, that you can do your stuff right, you don't talk in front of nobody if you're going to do some stuff, so you don't get caught for it," said Edwardo, a member of the Latin Kings, a Milwaukee gang.[4]

Sometimes a new member has to fight older, stronger members to prove he is brave enough to be in a gang. This is particularly true of the Mexican-American gangs of the Southwest. Author Luis Rodriguez tells of being "jumped" into a gang in his book *Always Running, Gang Days in L.A.* Rodriguez, then fourteen, had been associating with a neighborhood gang, but he was not officially a member. When he attended a party in his neighborhood, one of his friends told him that new members would be "jumped in" later that night. His friend told him that they would not hurt him very much. The friend was mistaken. Rodriguez told of being brutally beaten by *veteranos* or older gang members to see if he had the spirit to be a gang member.[5]

Chinese gangs often recruit members from junior and senior high schools. David Chong, an officer in the New York Police Department who went undercover in the Flying Dragon gang of New York City, described the process.

> I would have my kids go to a high school in Chinatown and look for the turkey right off the boat . . . and tease him, beat him up, knock him around. We isolate this kid; he's our target. What will happen, one day I'll make sure I'm around when this kid is getting beaten up, and I'll stop it with the snap of my finger. . . . I'm going to be this kid's hero, this kid's guru. . . . I'll take him to a safe house where I keep kids and guns. Then I slowly break him in.[6]

Identification with the Gang

Once a member has joined a gang, he may get a tattoo and adopt the dress of the gang. Tattoos show a total, lifelong commitment to the gang. After joining a Chinese gang, Sonny Wong, a sixteen-year-old gang member in New York City, had his chest and arms tattooed with green dragons and an eagle. He also copied the dress of other members of the gang—a black jacket, black turtleneck, tight black jeans, and black canvas slippers without socks. In that gang, male members also liked to have their hair permed and streaked with red, yellow, and green dye.[7]

Many gang members wear jackets associated with the local sports teams. In Los Angeles, jackets and other gear from the Los Angeles Raiders are popular. Some Crips wear British Knight-brand athletic shoes because to them the logo, BK, stands for Blood Killer.

Gang members like to strut around school and brag about their activities, such as their drug and drinking parties. In poor neighborhoods, they also like to show off the spoils of their illegal activities. Wearing expensive gold jewelry, clip-on gold teeth, designer clothing and beepers can be an indication of gang involvement.[8]

Graffiti and Monikers

Gangs use symbols that communicate meanings that ordinary people often cannot decode. They write these symbols on walls, using marking pens or spray paint, or they use hand signals to communicate with one another. These symbols reinforce their sense of togetherness and set them apart from other groups.

In Chicago, the symbols of gangs such as the Black Gangster Disciples include a six-pointed star and a pitchfork. The gangs of the rival People Nation, such as the Vice Lords, have a five-pointed star.[9]

"Cuz," "cuzz," or "cuzzin" indicates Crip graffiti. Writing "187," the number of the California penal code for homicide, means murder.[10]

Gang members also are known by their street names, or monikers. Some examples of common street names

Gang members see graffiti as a way to communicate messages to each other that will not be understood by outsiders.

used by Hispanic gangs are Loco (Crazy), Ghost, Droopy, or Flaco (Skinny). Author Luis Rodriguez was called Chin because he has a prominent jaw. Some of the African-American gang monikers mentioned in Leon Bing's book, *Do or Die*, are G-Roc, Monster, and Cyco-Mike.

Gang members write their names on walls, freeway overpasses, and buildings. Gang graffiti contains block letters and is difficult for outsiders to decipher. Graffiti indicates the name of the gang in power in a neighborhood and the names of members of the gang. Crossing out a member's name or a gang name is considered disrespectful. The Los Angeles Crip will not use the letter B, because they hate Bloods. The Bloods will use K instead of C in their graffiti to show their disrespect for Crips. In Chicago, graffiti written upside down constitutes an insult. FK, written upside down stands for Folk Killer. A pitchfork painted upside down is a challenge from the Vice Lords.

Gang Communication

It is important for a gang member to look tough. One way to accomplish this is through body language. Some gang members walk in a methodical, deliberate manner. They may stare at an opponent in a challenging manner.

Gang members communicate with one another through hand signals, expressions, and body language. Gang language is constantly changing. Some of the words and expressions used by gang members twist and change into new meanings. As expressions become

Gang names are called monikers or in the case of Hispanic gangs, *placas*. In this graffiti, "Droops" is the name of the gang member who made the graffiti. The letters are initials of his gang.

accepted, they begin to appear in conversations of nongang members.

Gang hand signals send messages that are difficult for outsiders to decipher. Some gangs have special handshakes. Like verbal language, hand signs change meanings, and new signs may take the place of the old. Hand signals may also challenge members of a rival gang. Often, when warring sets or gangs throw hand signs, a fight may follow. Misreading body signals can result in a fight or drive-by shooting. Often innocent people get hurt.

José Roman, twenty-one, was walking along on a Chicago street on March 28, 1992, when two gang members in a stolen car pulled alongside and flashed hand signals of another gang. Police said that this is a common tactic to trick rivals. Although Roman did not belong to a gang, he flashed the hand sign back for his protection. When the teenagers fired at him with a shotgun, pellets lodged in his brain, permanently disabling him.[11]

Gang Leadership

Like any other group, gangs have leaders who determine much of what goes on in the gang. Sometimes, the leadership is formal. Other times, it is informal and changes frequently.

The Chinese gangs of New York City are headed by a *dai lo*, which is a term of respect for a leader or boss. Some of the gangs even have a bigger boss than the *dai lo*. Behind the Green Dragon gang was a boss who was much older than most of the members. Born in 1955, he had become a millionaire selling heroin and other drugs as well as smuggling illegal immigrants into the United States. The younger members of the Green Dragons gave him status and provided him with bodyguards.[12]

In his book, *The Compound,* author William Gale tells how five gangs of approximately 700 African-American and Puerto Rican youths stormed a middle-class complex in the South Bronx in the early 1970s, turning the building into a fortress called "The Compound." During the time they occupied The Compound, the gangs committed many beatings, gang rapes, and four murders.

Leadership in The Compound was organized and structured. Big Mama was the head of the girls' division of the Savage Nomads, one of the gangs living in The Compound. Her husband, Black Bongo, was the supreme leader of the Savage Nomads.[13]

They not only ruled over their own gang, but the other gangs also respected them. No outside gang could visit The Compound without their approval.[14]

Leadership in many gangs, however, is not this structured and formal. Sergeant Wes McBride, director of Operation Safe Streets, of the Los Angeles Sheriff's Department, says that in many gangs leadership is assumed by one or more individuals. "A gang may have ten to fifteen members who might have the 'juice' to be leaders," he said.[15]

Older gang members who have built reputations are treated with respect. Hispanic gangs have their "veterano" who is an older gang member, usually in his twenties, who is still active in the gang without being involved in combat. In African-American gangs, an O.G.,

70

or original gangster, is a member who is held in awe because he has a reputation as a fighter. Although these men are treated with honor, they exert little influence over younger members.[16]

Gang Fighting

Gang fights have always been a dangerous by-product of gang life. Gang members fight for power, respect, and revenge and to defend their turf. "A gang-banger's manner, speech, dress, and actions—even his car—are all part of an elaborate set of rituals that convey status and respect, and respect is worth dying for," writes author William Broyles, Jr.[17]

Looking tough and acting crazy are ways a gang member gains a reputation, or rep. Having a rep can make a person a target for rivals who are seeking to expand their own reputations. In the past, gang members fought with fists, brass knuckles, chains, and knives, but today guns are the weapon of choice. Gang fights are more violent than ever.

Gangbangs, or fights, are also social happenings. How a person reacts in a gangbang is a topic of conversation. Fights can be planned, can come when one gang ambushes another as retaliation, or can be a spontaneous incident or result of a perceived insult to an individual or to the gang.[18]

Gang Membership and Life Outside the Gang

Many gang members have a history of low achievement and discipline problems at school. After joining a gang, young people who have not had these problems in the past often change their behavior. Gang members may cut school and develop a pattern of truancy. Some members get into fights with other students or teachers and cause trouble in class.

At home, they may be unwilling to attend family gatherings and may not want to attend church services with their families. Besides withdrawing from family members, they may want to stay out later than usual. It is not unusual for young people involved in gangs to drink alcohol and use drugs.

The gang becomes more important than anything else, and it is important to be loyal to the gang. Because the values of the gang have become more important than those of his or her family, the hard-core gang member will do whatever the gang wants. Personal goals for the future are not as important as the desires of the gang.

One gang member in jail wrote of how he got caught up in his gang:

> I started causing trouble as soon as I entered junior high school . . . ditching, burglarizing homes, stealing cars, and drinking just to impress the homeboys and prove that I wasn't a punk. Yeah, you are probably gonna say that homeboys will help you out. But they still put lots of pressure on you. Testing you. Seeing if you are down for the varrio.[19]

Leaving the Gang

Once in a gang, a young person may find it is very difficult to leave because one cannot simply resign membership in the gang. Tammy Membreno, director of the Barrio Action Group in the El Sereno district of East Los Angeles, described the difficulties of leaving the gang.

> You can't go to the gang and say, 'I think I've had enough. I want to leave.' If you're a detriment to other gang members, if they don't like you, they may jump you out. You would be someone who doesn't hang out with the boys, who don't do the kind of activities a gang member does. They will initiate a jump out whether a guy wants it or not. Usually the person who is jumped out is a person who is not a traditional gang member. He might be fat and wouldn't be a good backup, if people starting running. They might not want someone who is 'goofy.' A jump out is big time. Some kids might be sent to the hospital after a jump out.

She said the gang might be more accepting if a person becomes religious and wants to leave on that account.[20] That is not always true, however. After eight months of gang-banging, Keith Smith, a minister's son in Waukegan, Illinois, decided to leave his gang. He had to fight four against one for three minutes. Although weapons were not used, Smith collapsed after one minute and remained in a coma for fifty-eight days.[21]

Some gang members say that the safest way to leave the gang is to fade away from its activities. Going into military service, playing athletics, or getting a chance to go to college are sometimes acceptable reasons for leaving. But for some unfortunate young people, the only way to get out of the gang is through death. Father Gregory J. Boyle, a priest who worked with gang members in East Los Angeles, said that gang members appear to almost seek death through dangerous activities. Some gang members would tell him, "You got to die sometimes."[22]

Gang funerals are elaborate rites. Some gang members are buried in homeboy attire. Floral arrangements may bear ribbons that say, "We love you homie." Sometimes, members wear custom-designed tee-shirts printed with messages honoring their dead friend. Sometimes funerals turn into gang battles. In one incident, gang members invaded a mortuary and stabbed a corpse. In another, as the funeral procession passed through enemy territory, armed gang members were waiting. The funeral caravan turned back.[23]

Even if a person survives leaving a gang, a part of his or her personality may remain gang-like if the reasons for joining have not been resolved. "Unfortunately, the ghost in the darkness always follows the gang member," Tammy Membreno said.

7

Gangs and Criminal Behavior

Violent acts and other criminal behavior have always been dangerous by-products of gang activities. Today, easy access to guns has made gang violence even more deadly than in the past. Gang members are not the only victims of gang violence. Innocent bystanders also get caught in the cross fire. One can simply look at the newspapers across the country to see the toll of gang violence.

In New York City, an eighteen-year-old suspected drug dealer was charged with systematically slaying six people execution-style on Valentine's Day, 1993. Neighbors said the apartment building where the killings occurred is in a part of the South Bronx where rival drug gangs are feuding over turf.[1] In Chicago, a thirteen-year-old boy was murdered two doors from his home as he said good night to his girlfriend. Police suspected that he

Today, gang members have access to highly sophisticated weapons, many equaling those of law-enforcement agencies. Some of the weapons include semi-automatic and automatic guns and rifles and vicious knives and machetes like these seized and later destroyed by the Los Angeles County Sheriff's Department. There are close to 120,000 gang members in Los Angeles County.

was mistaken for someone else in a battle over gang rivalries and drug dealing. "The teenagers are killing everybody," one of his friends, age eleven, said. "They don't care."[2]

Large cities are not the only scenes of gang violence. Smaller towns and suburbs are also experiencing a rash of gang crime. In Little Rock, Arkansas, an eighteen-year-old was slain when he traded opposing hand signals with the occupants of an open car. The chief prosecutor of the county said his office had identified forty-one named gangs in the area, most involving young black men. There were also several female gangs and a few white gangs.[3]

Authorities in South Lake Tahoe, a mountain resort town located on the California-Nevada border, believe that gang members from Los Angeles and the San Joaquin Valley have come to the area to recruit low-income Filipino and Latino youth. Rivalry between the two best-known gangs, the South Side 13 and Bahala Na Gang (BNG), escalated into violence when one gangbanger threw a bottle at a carload of BNGs. A few nights later, during a fight between the two gangs, a seventeen-year-old was shot in the back as he tried to escape.[4]

Gang Violence Results in Deaths

In Los Angeles County, an area with a serious gang problem, the rate of gang-related homicides has soared dramatically since 1984 when there were 212 gang-related slayings. This accounted for 21 percent of all murders in the county. In 1991, the 771 gang-related killings accounted for 38 percent of the total homicides.

By 1992, the number had risen to 803. Nearly two-thirds of the gang-related fatalities involved violence among Latino gangs, especially those gangs formed from Mexico and Central America immigrants. Officials predicted that the gang-related deaths could soon reach 1,000 per year.[5]

Drive-by shootings and other fighting usually involves small sets or groups of gang members, not the entire gang. Violence escalates as members seek revenge. One gang war between two rival Crips sets has lasted for over twelve years, and more than two dozen people have been killed. The hostilities began with a rivalry over a junior-high-school romance.

Drive-by shootings are a serious public health problem in inner-city Los Angeles, according to a report printed in *The New England Journal of Medicine*. Gangs use drive-by shootings to terrorize members of rival gangs. The Los Angeles Police Department defines a drive-by shooting as a gang-related or gang-motivated incident in which a suspect or suspects shoot at individuals or an occupied dwelling from a vehicle, resulting in a homicide, attempted murder, or assault. It is estimated that more than 90 percent of such shootings are caused by members of street gangs. In 1991, 2,222 people were shot in 1,548 drive-by shootings in Los Angeles. Of these, 583 incidents involved 677 juveniles under the age of eighteen and 429 of these had firearm injuries. Of those actually shot, 76 percent were Latino, and 22 percent were African-American. Eighty-six percent were males. Statistics also revealed that of the 429 children and adolescents injured, 303, or 71 percent, were documented members of violent street gangs.[6]

Many of the homicide victims were young teens between the ages of thirteen and sixteen. Since 1991, when the Los Angeles County coroner's office began computerizing their statistics, 46 youths between thirteen and sixteen have been killed. During the first six months of 1994, 49 homicides were reported in this age group. Although nationwide the overall crime rate of incidents reported to the police dropped 3 percent in 1993, the killing of teens has increased 55 percent since 1988. According to the FBI, there were 2,500 juvenile homicides reported in the United States in 1992.[7]

Nationwide, the 1991 Uniform Crime Report of the Federal Bureau of Investigations, Department of Justice, noted an upsurge in the juvenile murder arrest rate during the 1980s. Although not all juvenile murder arrests involve gang members, it is fair to estimate that a number of them are gang-related. From 1965 to 1990, the overall juvenile crime rate increased 322 percent

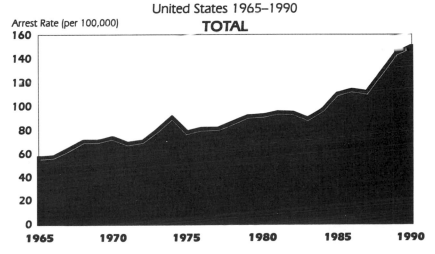

JUVENILE WEAPON VIOLATIONS ARREST RATES
United States 1965–1990

Arrest Rate (per 100,000)

TOTAL

from 2.8 to 12.1. In the 1980s, the report states, there was a 79-percent increase in the number of murders committed using guns.

Although the murder arrest rate for all juveniles rose during the 1980s, the most dramatic increase occurred with African-American juveniles. In this group, the rate between 1980 and 1990 increased 145 percent.

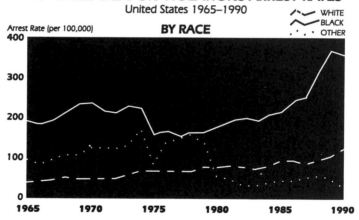

JUVENILE WEAPON VIOLATIONS ARREST RATES
United States 1965–1990

It is interesting to look at the statistics involving weapon law violations by juveniles. In 1990, there were 151 arrests for every 100,000 juveniles for weapon law violations. The arrest rate for white youth rose 58 percent; for African Americans, the increase was 103 percent. Because they make up a large percentage of the United States population, whites still accounted for a greater number (62 percent) of actual weapon-related arrests. Blacks accounted for 36 percent.[8]

Far more gang members, both male and female, commit crimes than do the rest of society. It is estimated

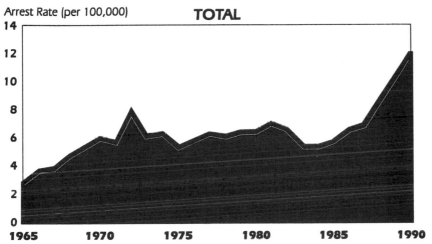

JUVENILE MURDER ARREST RATES
United States 1965–1990

Arrest Rate (per 100,000)   **TOTAL**

that male gang members are responsible for more than six times as much crime as nongang members and that more than half of all gang members (56 percent) have committed more than one crime. Gang violence is driven in part by the desire of younger members to match the reputations of older members.[9]

Causes of Gang Violence

A report published by the Los Angeles County district attorney's office in 1992, titled *Gangs, Crime and Violence in L.A.*, says that fighting, partying, and unemployment are the most important causes of gang violence. Fights over turf and status and for revenge account for most gang-related homicides. Fights occur when someone threatens a gang member's reputation. If a member has a tough reputation, fewer people will bother him.[10]

In his book, *Islands in the Street,* professor Martin Sanchez Jankowski quotes Cone, a nineteen-year-old gang member from New York:

> You see, if you ain't got respect and a reputation, then people be messing with you and taking your women and stuff like that, you know stuff you have to fight over. Plus if people don't respect you, they won't hang [hang out] with you either.[11]

Gang members are often proud of the scars they receive in fights because these show their bravery and loyalty to the gang. They also revere those members who have been killed while defending the honor of the gang.[12]

Violence may also be caused by physical factors such as poor diet, lack of sleep, and drug and alcohol abuse. Most gang members do not have access to large amounts of money needed for drugs. Many do not have the skills to find work. Frequently, they turn to crime for profits. They may deal drugs or commit thefts and armed robberies and burglaries. Cash from drug deals also makes it easier for gang members to buy more dangerous weapons, which in turn breed violence.[13]

Gangs and Drugs

Much has been written about gangs and drugs. For many years, gangs have been involved with narcotics. In New York City in the early 1960s, young people took drugs to escape the boredom, despair, and hopelessness of living in poverty. They used liquor, marijuana, and heroin. Some sniffed model airplane glue in bags. Although heroin users continued to be included in gang

GANG-RELATED CRIME BY TYPE
AS PERCENT OF TOTAL RECORDED

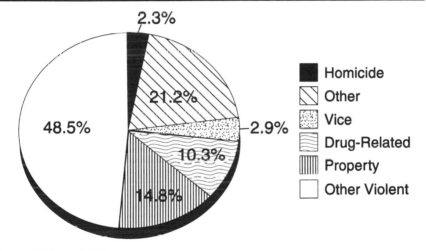

Source: NIJ Gang Survey

Gang-related crime is above all a violent crime problem. Homicides and other violent crimes account for about half of all recorded gang-related crime incidents. Crimes more related to profit, such as property crimes, drug-related crimes and vice, represent comparatively smaller portions of the national gang crime problem.

activities, most of the gang leaders were against heroin use because once someone was hooked, he became more or less useless as a fighter. He would spend much of his time hustling to get dope. Authorities in New York and other large cities such as Philadelphia, Chicago, and Los Angeles began to see that when there was more drug use, gang activity declined.[14]

In the 1980s, however, drugs returned with a vengeance. In Chicago, African-American street gangs organized a network of drug distribution that brought high profits. As the demand for drugs increased, gangs became more violent in their desire to control the market.[15]

In some large high-rise housing projects, small groups would take control of the project elevators to control drug sales.[16]

In Los Angeles, more gang members use drugs and alcohol than do nongang youth. It is estimated that over 70 percent use drugs at least once a week. Black gangs prefer cocaine, especially crack. Hispanic gangs use P.C.P. or "angel dust." Chinese gangs are most likely to use opium and heroin. White motorcycle gangs prefer methamphetamine or speed. Marijuana is commonly used in all the different groups. Although gangs use drugs, they frown upon addiction. Heroin is looked down upon because it threatens the member's loyalty to the gang.

According to the Los Angeles County district attorney's office, although approximately half of all gang members may sell drugs in any given year, only one out of seven sells regularly. Most are small-time drug dealers.[17]

The arrival in Los Angeles of crack cocaine in the early 1980s caused an explosion of drug abuse. Although many gang members did become involved in distribution of crack, it has not been proven that gang members control the drug trade and the violence attached to it. Various studies indicate that drug use and sales by gang members were not major causes of gang-related homicides. Actually, narcotics were less a factor in killings involving gang members than in those homicides unrelated to gangs.[18]

Drugs, Unemployment, and the Older Gang Member

In the past, young people would leave the gang as they reached their early twenties. Some would join the military. Others would get married or find a job. Today, these options are harder to come by. The military is much more selective as to whom they admit for service. Usually, gang members are poor students. Many have dropped out of school. Their skills are very poor. Finding a job is difficult. As gang members grow older, selling drugs and stolen weapons and committing other small crimes becomes a way to survive on the streets. Most of these individuals are small operators.

James H. Hagedorn, who interviewed gang members in Milwaukee, found that of those he questioned twenty-one said that they sold drugs now and then, eight said they sold regularly, and two admitted to being dealers. They obtained drugs for others to sell. Hagedorn concluded that the majority of the Milwaukee gang members lacked the organization to move into organized crime. He did, however, note that the lack of good full-time jobs might encourage some to move into expanded drug sales.[19]

The Los Angeles County district attorney's office found that violence for profit was on the increase among older gang members, especially where drugs were concerned. Their evidence shows that although younger gang members in their teens were primarily involved in violence related to status and turf, older members were moving into mid-level drug dealing. As more and more people compete in the drug marketplace, there is more conflict and greater possibility of violence.

We have seen how violent and criminal acts are part of the daily life of gang members. Sooner or later, the gang member will be arrested for breaking the law. The next chapter looks at what happens when a gang member is arrested and enters the justice system.

---|8|

Arrest, Trial, and Prison

A gang member who repeatedly breaks the law will probably end up in the criminal justice system. Depending on the circumstances of the offense, after the arrest he or she may be detained and go through a preliminary hearing and a trial. If found guilty, the person may have to pay a fine, be placed on probation, or serve time in a detention or correctional institution. Treatment of prisoners varies from state to state. Those under the age of eighteen are usually tried as juveniles.

The Juvenile System

The objective of the juvenile court is rehabilitation of the young offender.[1] In many states, the law protects juveniles by keeping their records confidential. It has long been considered inappropriate to put young people in prison alongside adults. As early as 1824, the state of

New York established the New York House of Refuge in New York City to help rehabilitate and reform children who had committed crimes. By 1990, most states had separate correctional facilities called reformatories or training schools for juvenile criminals.

The first juvenile court was established in Illinois in 1899. In 1905, a court case in Pennsylvania denied children the right to trial by jury because it was reasoned that young people were not brought to court to be tried but to be saved. As time went on, the juvenile justice system began to take on aspects of the adult courts. New York's Family Court Act of 1962 provided for the appointment of an attorney for all juveniles appearing before the court. Five years later, the Supreme Court decision called *In Re Gault* made the appointment of an attorney a constitutional requirement for all juvenile delinquency cases.

As the criminal acts of juveniles became more and more serious, there were calls to treat young offenders as adults. In 1976, the New York legislature passed the Juvenile Justice Reform Act. This act stated that although the needs and interests of the juvenile offender should be considered, there should also be consideration of protecting the community from violent offenders. In 1978, New York established the category of juvenile offender. A juvenile offender is a juvenile who commits serious crimes such as murder, rape, robbery, or arson.[2]

Treatment of juveniles differs from state to state. Often, juveniles may be sentenced to spend time in a secured institution training school, camp, or ranch. Training schools are more secure than ranches or camps because they restrict the inmate's movements and privileges. Some young offenders are sent to group homes that are managed by live-in counselors.[3]

Unfortunately, after they are released from these less-harsh facilities, many young offenders are later convicted of new crimes. For example, a study of the California Youth Authority found that 43 percent of juveniles released from Los Angeles County Probation Department camps are later convicted of new crimes.[4] Gang members may consider going to jail a badge of honor. Time spent in jail or a youth authority facility may bring a higher status in the gang. Gang associations also continue within the youth facility.

Because younger gang members receive lighter sentences, they are sometimes chosen to commit more serious offenses for the gang. A nineteen-year-old gang member in New York told younger members not to worry about jail. ". . . I tell them, hey, the courts is on your side. You're too young to get jail on your first bust, and even after that you so young you won't spend hardly no time in jail."[5]

In the case of a very serious crime such as murder, rape, or arson, the juvenile court may determine that a juvenile may be tried as an adult. His or her case is waived to the adult court system.

The Adult System

The case is sent to a prosecutor, an attorney who represents the interest of the public. At that time, the crime is given a classification of misdemeanor or felony. Misdemeanors include minor crimes such as shoplifting, being drunk in public, or smoking marijuana. Felonies are much more serious crimes such as rape, assault, burglary, armed robbery, or murder. A person found guilty of a felony may have to spend more than a year in a local jail or a state prison. He or she may also lose the right to vote and the right to hold political office.

The prosecutor schedules a preliminary hearing in which the accused is read his or her rights and is asked to submit a plea of guilty or not guilty. If the defendant does not have money to hire an attorney, a court-appointed attorney, or public defender, is assigned to the case. If there is doubt about the evidence, the hearing may take place in a private session before a grand jury.

After the preliminary hearing, a trial date is scheduled, and bail is determined. Bail refers to money put up by the accused so that he or she may be released from jail before the trial. People who "skip bail," or leave before the trial, forfeit or lose the bail money. The judge determines the amount of money needed for bail. If the court fears that the defendant may run away, bail may be denied, and the defendant will remain in jail until the trial.

In some cases, the defense lawyer and the prosecutor meet to try to settle the case without going to trial. This is called plea bargaining. If a decision cannot be reached through plea bargaining, the case goes to trial, and both sides present their arguments. Some defendants choose to have their case heard before a judge who will determine their guilt or innocence. If the defendant chooses a trial by jury, the jury must decide that the person is guilty beyond a reasonable doubt. If judged guilty, the person must return to the court for sentencing. The sentence could be paying a fine, probation, or going to prison. Sometimes the sentence is a combination of these. If the crime is very serious, the person may be sentenced to life in prison or even death.[6]

Although the justice system in the United States attempts to treat all people alike, in fact, there are some inequalities. Social scientists who have studied criminal statistics also point out that many factors such as race, personal appearance, and place of residence affect whether or not a person is likely to be arrested and brought before the criminal court.[7] Because many gang members are poor and from minority groups, they are also affected by these biases.

Community Service Probation and Other Alternatives to Prison

After a person is found guilty of a crime, he or she is sentenced. Usually, if the person does not have a criminal record or if the crime is a minor one, he or she may be required to do community service, which means working a certain number of hours to benefit the community. The idea behind this is that the entire community is hurt by acts of crime, and public service helps to pay back the community. In some states, people who are guilty of minor crimes may have their arrest and conviction removed from the records after they successfully complete public service orders.

Probation allows the offender to remain at liberty while under the supervision of a probation officer. Under the rules of probation, the person must regularly check in for counseling so that the officer can see if the terms of probation are being kept. Some of the requirements of probation may include holding a job or attending school regularly, not being involved in drugs and alcohol, and keeping away from criminals.

Sometimes restitution is a condition of probation. Restitution means paying the victim equivalent value for damage caused by the offenses committed by the criminal. Offenders may meet with victims to decide on the amount of money or the services needed to make restitution. The probation officer acts as a go-between.[8] In some cases, the offender may perform service for the victim to make up for the loss.[9] In other cases, the court may set an amount, collect it, and distribute it to the victim.

Prison

Because many of the serious crimes committed by juvenile gang members require them to undergo trial in the adult system, their sentence may involve serving a term in a state prison. Prisons or correctional institutions are different from jails. Jails are used to hold people accused of breaking the law until they can come to trial. People who have committed minor offenses or misdemeanors such as being drunk in public or those who have received shorter sentences may also be housed in jails.[10]

Prisons are used to hold convicted criminals while they serve out their sentences. Prisons differ from state to state. Prisoners convicted of nonviolent or less serious offenses and who are not likely to escape are housed in minimum-security prisons where rules are not as strict as they are in medium-security and maximum-security prisons where there are more walls, more guards, and many

Many gang members who break the law end up in a state prison where their lives are highly restricted. Gangs also operate in prison. Members of prison gangs who become violent and cause trouble may end up in a prison block such as these located in Pelican Bay, a maximum-security prison in northern California.

restrictions. Sometimes, there are several levels of security within the same prison complex.[11]

Inmates find that in prison someone else will be making most of the decisions about their lives. The main feature of life in prison is routine and repetition. Prisons suppress freedom, privacy, and individuality. Prisons are crowded. When people live very close to one another, hostility often takes the form of personal conflicts and gang violence.[12] Being in prison is very dangerous because crime flourishes. Studies show that the homicide rate in prison is higher than that in the general population.

For some convicts, allegiance to the outside gang continues in prison. The convict may also join a prison gang such as the Mexican Mafia, the Black Muslims, or the Aryan Brotherhood.[13]

Most states do try to offer inmates training and employment in the prison. In California, prisoners manufacture all the clothing, shoes, jackets, and other apparel they wear. They harvest crops, cook food, and learn job skills, such as grinding lenses for eyeglasses and word processing. Inmates can also work to finish high school and some even take college courses.[14] Still, years spent in prison represent a tragic loss of productive years.

Rene Hernandez was sentenced a long term in a California prison because of activities that evolved from gang membership. His words describe the tragic outcome of joining a gang:

> I was about 13 years old when I joined a gang. I am now 25, and I have spent the better part of those years in and out of prison, not to mention

Prisoners face a life of broken dreams, as seen in this drawing by an inmate. He writes, "There is no room at all in which to experience any spaciousness or openness. Fight for life cuz without life our dreams won't exist."

hospitals. This is not exactly what I had in mind when I joined a gang.

Sitting here, surrounded by these unforgiving walls of concrete, I often find myself drifting in memories in order to escape the cruel reality of prison life. What's sad is that the memories are filled with senseless hate, violence, drugs and crime. I used to belong to a gang, and unfortunately, that's where most of my memories come from. Once you join a gang, you become part of it. You belong to it. You do as they do and as they say, and there's no easy way out.

Needless to say, I am in prison now with a long sentence because of gangs. Is there any doubt that gangs are no good? Gangs will lead you nowhere, and if anywhere, it will be prison or the morgue.[15]

9

Gangs—Breaking the Cycle of Violence

There are many victims of gang violence. Some are young people who become so caught up in the gang lifestyle that they are unable to lead productive adult lives in society. Other victims are innocent people caught up in the violence of gang rivalries.

Three young teenagers from Pomona, California, are examples of innocent bystanders whose lives were changed by gangs even though they were not members themselves. When a friend who was a gang member was killed in a drive-by shooting, the three teens—two of them fourteen and one sixteen—were able to identify the killer who was from a rival gang. Their testimony led to his conviction. Members of his gang later murdered one of the youths in retaliation. The other two boys live in fear of the same fate.[1]

Schools are no longer safe havens. In a Los Angeles

high school, a local gang claimed a specific public telephone booth as its turf. When a nongang member used it, an argument broke out. In the fight that followed, the student was killed. Thirty-five students withdrew from school out of fear.[2]

The community at large is also a victim of gang activity. Graffiti-covered buildings must be cleaned up regularly, and gunshots in the night cause fear. Fear of gangs has led residents in many communities to hire patrols and demand that their neighborhoods be guarded. In downtown Seattle, Portland, and Tacoma, business owners have hired private security patrols to police large sections of the downtown streets to discourage gang members from gathering.[3]

In many areas of Los Angeles, homeowners have petitioned the city to barricade public streets. In Athens Heights, a neighborhood of South Central Los Angeles, neighbors petitioned the city for gates and barricades to keep gang members out. After being installed, crime declined. Chicago Mayor Richard Daley has suggested a similar solution in some of the areas of his city.[4]

Programs to Keep Kids out of Gangs

Most social workers believe that programs targeting at-risk youngsters who have not yet joined a gang is the most effective approach. The Boys and Girls Clubs of America, in conjunction with the U.S. Department of Justice, has developed an intervention program called Targeted Outreach. Through their referral network with courts, police, other juvenile justice agencies, schools, social service agencies, and community organizations,

Community groups use murals and billboards to put across the message that gang violence must be stopped. They are aware that gang warfare destroys the fabric of a community.

young people who are identified as being at-risk are recruited into club activities to divert them from joining a gang. Boys and Girls Clubs of America make a major effort to reach boys and girls living in public housing projects.

In a pilot program during 1990 and 1991, over 1,900 young people on the brink of gang involvement were enrolled in programs at thirty-three clubs nationwide. At the end of the one-year project, 48 percent of the youth had improved their school behavior and 33 percent had improved their grades. The young people participate in programs that encourage leadership, physical fitness, drug and alcohol prevention, and cultural enrichment.[5]

The program of the Kips Bay Boys and Girls Club in the South Bronx reaches 4,500 youths in a drug- and gang-infested neighborhood. Many children have friends and relatives who have been shot and stabbed. One of the most active members, Rafael Moore, a parentless boy, was rescued from the streets by the club's unit director, Frank Sanchez, Jr., "I've tried to take the role of the parents Rafael doesn't have," Sanchez said.[6]

The Los Angeles Police Department operates three boxing rings located in the areas of the city where Hispanic gangs are active. Volunteer coaches give pointers on boxing technique, and youngsters from eight to eighteen come after school to practice and work out on exercise machines. Because of the popularity of the sport in Hispanic communities, boxing is an accepted diversion from gang activity. Young people are not turned away if they are gang members. Because of the sponsorship of the police, the program is considered a safe haven. It also provides an acceptable way to work out energy and aggression in a neutral area.[7]

Education as a Solution

Because many gang members have low school achievement and may be high school dropouts, education is used as a tool in rehabilitation. Edgemont Center in the Upper Manhattan neighborhood of Washington Heights is a daytime high security facility operated by the probation department to educate young, often violent offenders who are on probation. It is a last step before being sent to prison. The program includes drug rehabilitation and remedial classes in reading and math. The probationers report to the center for eight and one-half hours a day, five days a week, while continuing to live at home. Treatment at the center costs the state approximately $4,000 a year compared with over $59,000 to keep a prisoner in jail for the same time.[8]

In Arizona, studies showed that 65 percent of criminals on probation were high school dropouts and 10 percent could barely read. Computerized learning centers located in state probation offices have helped offenders prepare for high school equivalency diplomas while they work at their own pace. Studies indicate that those who take the program are more likely to successfully complete probation.[9]

Paramount, California, is a city with a serious gang problem. There are multigenerational Hispanic gangs, a gang of immigrant youths, a Crip clique, and several tagger groups. The city was one of the first to include a course in gang prevention in the school curriculum. In

Many programs have discovered that teaching gang members and offenders job skills helps them become productive members of society. These young women prisoners are learning word processing to help them find jobs. Many gang members and juvenile offenders are high school dropouts.

ten years, more than 9,000 students in the second, fifth, and seventh grades have taken the fifteen-hour course called Alternatives to Gang Membership. Ninety-eight percent of the graduates of the course have stayed away from gangs.[10]

Parent education is also a strong factor in helping families keep their children away from gangs. Mary Thomas is a good example of how a dedicated single parent can keep her children from joining a gang. When gang members tried to recruit her children, she confronted them.

"She was very heavy handed as a mother and we were well disciplined," said her son, basketball great, Isiah Thomas.

In spite of her discipline, she also expressed a lot of love toward her children. "No matter how many mistakes I made, she always was there to say, 'I care and I want you to make it!' I always had someone I could go to if things got rough," said her other son, Mark Thomas, a Chicago police officer.[11]

Helping Hardcore Gang Members

Once a person is heavily involved in a gang, it becomes increasingly harder to change the course of his or her life. In some cities, counselors must take to the streets to talk gang members out of violent confrontations. They also help those who want to begin the process of leaving the gang lifestyle.

In Los Angeles, an agency called Community Youth Gang Services was created in 1981, with funding from both Los Angeles County and the city of Los Angeles.

The counselors, some of them former gang members, go to gang neighborhoods with the philosophy that young people in gangs can be rehabilitated. A twenty-four-hour crisis hot line helps settle gang-related disputes. To offer an alternative to joining a gang, their program includes training for job interviews to help at-risk youth obtain jobs, graffiti removal, and a fifteen-week elementary school course that teaches about the negative aspects of gangs and alternatives to joining one. They also attempt to work out peace agreements between rival gangs during holiday season.[12]

Gang Truces

Gang members themselves often see the futility of violence. The awareness that they have been killing other young people of the same race leads some older gang members to attempt truces and peace treaties. One of the largest truces occurred after the Los Angeles riots in the spring of 1992. One group, Hands Across Watts, has helped maintain peace in the Watts housing projects. The truce produced several success stories.

One member, Charles Rachel, an inactive member of the 5 Duce Broadway Crips, was invited to President Clinton's inauguration in January 1993. Hi-I, a member of the Grape Street Watts Crips, has obtained private financing to open a sporting goods store in a riot-torn neighborhood of South-Central Los Angeles. His business employs twelve people.

Truce movements between black gangs in Watts, Boston, Chicago, Minneapolis, and Philadelphia have had some effect on stopping the killing, but they have not been strong enough to make a large impact. Efforts to form a truce have been unsuccessful with Hispanic gangs that are numerous and violent.[13]

A group of Hispanic gang leaders from Los Angeles County *barrios* did meet in August 1992 to discuss the self-destructive cycle of gang violence. "Let's stop killing our own *raza*" (race), proclaimed a banner at the conference. Below was a picture of a gang member cradling a dying friend in a pool of blood. Unfortunately, of more than 500 Latino gangs in Los Angeles County, fewer than a dozen attended.[14]

Conclusion

The bloody cycle of gangs and gang warfare will probably continue until the social problems that cause them are resolved. Most experts, whether in law enforcement or social work, and older gang members agree that only deep social and economic changes can really make a difference.

Now you know a lot about gangs, the reasons why people join them, and the problems they cause. What do you think about gangs? How can you and your friends help young people keep away from gang involvement? What can communities and schools do to keep young people in school and direct gangs toward less dangerous activities?

Other Resources

Juvenile Justice Clearinghouse/NCJRS
Box 6000
Rockville, MD 20849-6000
800-638-8736

This agency, sponsored by the Office of Juvenile Justice and Delinquency Prevention, U.S. Department of Justice, collects and disseminates information about a wide range of gang-related subjects. The center has a library of gang-related documents about gang prevention and intervention and produce a comprehensive bibliography of gang-related books and articles.

The National School Safety Center
4165 Thousand Oaks Blvd., Suite 290
Westlake Village, CA 91362
805-373-9977

This agency is a partnership cosponsored by Pepperdine University, the U.S. Department of Justice, and the U.S. Department of Education. It tracks issues of school safety, including information on gangs in schools.

Boys and Girls Clubs of America
1230 W. Peachtree St. NW
Atlanta, GA 30309-3447
404-815-5700

The Boys and Girls Clubs is a nationwide federation of youth-serving agencies with a primary mission of service to boys and girls from disadvantaged backgrounds. There are approximately 1,450 clubs and facilities throughout the United States serving approximately 1.8 million youth ranging in age from six to eighteen. The clubs are actively involved in gang prevention and intervention.

Chapter Notes

Chapter 1

1. Eugene M. Methvin, "When the Gangs Came to Tacoma," *Reader's Digest* (May 1992), pp. 134–135.

2. Jim Herron Zamora, "Slain Youth's Dreams Die With Him," *Los Angeles Times* (August 27, 1992), p. B3.

3. Fredric Dannen, "The Revenge of the Green Dragons," *New Yorker* (November 18, 1991), pp. 103–105.

4. James Willwerth, "From Killing Fields to Mean Streets," *Time* (November 18, 1991), pp. 103–105.

5. "Gangs Active in 94% of U.S. Cities, USC Study Finds," *Los Angeles Times* (May 25, 1993), p. B2.

6. William Raspberry, "Losing Ground," *Newsweek* (April 6, 1992), pp. 20–21.

7. "In the Brutal World of L.A. Gangs—Author Leon Bing Talks about Gang Life in L.A.," *Time* (March 16, 1992), p. 16.

Chapter 2

1. "Teenage Terror on the New York Streets," *Life* (July 11, 1955), pp. 33–35.

2. Herbert Asbury, *The Gangs of New York: An Informal History of the Underworld* (New York: Knopf, 1927), pp. 9–22.

3. Ibid. pp. 28–29.

4. James Haskins, *Street Gangs Yesterday and Today* (New York: Hastings House, 1978), p. 31.

5. Asbury, pp. 61–64.

6. Haskins, pp. 61–64.

7. Useni Eugene Perkins, *Explosion of Chicago's Black Street Gangs: 1900 to Present* (Chicago: Third World Press, 1987), pp. 19–27.

8. *Gangs, Crime and Violence in L.A. 1992* (County of Los Angeles: Office of the District Attorney, May 1992), p. 4.

9. John D. Weaver, *L.A., El Pueblo Grande* (Pasadena, Calif.: Ward Ritchie Press, 1973), pp. 103–105.

10. Christopher Rand, *The Puerto Ricans* (New York: Oxford Press, 1958), p. 15.

11. R. Lincoln Keiser, *The Vice Lords, Warriors of the Streets* (New York: Holt, Rinehart and Winston, 1969), pp. vii, 1.

12. Ibid. pp. 105–107.

13. Haskins, pp. 105–107.

14. Martin Tolchin, "Gangs Spread Terror in the South Bronx," *New York Times* (January 15, 1973), pp. 1ff, and "South Bronx: A Jungle Stalked by Fear, Seized by Rage," *New York Times* (January 16, 1973), pp. 1ff.

15. William Gale, *The Compound* (New York: Rawson Associates, 1977), pp. 9–10.

Chapter 3

1. Ruth Horowitz, "Sociological Perspectives on Gangs, Conflicting Definitions and Concepts," *Gangs in America*, ed. C. Ronald Huff (Newbury Park, Calif.: Sage Publications, 1990), p. 44.

2. *Gang Prevention Through Targeted Outreach*, Boys and Girls Clubs of America, prepared under Grant No. 90-JD CX-K004 from the office of Juvenile Justice and Delinquency Prevention, Office of Justice Programs, U.S. Department of Justice, 1993, p. 4.

3. James Hagedorn, *People and Folk, Gangs, Crime and the*

Underclass in a Rustbelt City (Chicago: Lakeside Press, 1988), p. 57.

4. Ibid. pp. 57–58.

5. Ibid. p. 77.

6. "Gang membership crosses cultural, geographic bounds," *School Safety Update*, National School Safety Center News Service (November 1991), p. 2.

7. *Gangs, Crime and Violence in L.A. 1992* (County of Los Angeles: Office of the District Attorney, May 1992), p. xiii.

8. Leon Bing, *Do or Die* (New York: Harper Collins, 1991), p. xiv.

9. Christopher Rand, *The Puerto Ricans* (New York: Oxford Press, 1958), pp. 88–92.

10. Elena Padilla, *Up for Puerto Rico* (New York: Columbia University Press, 1958), pp. 230–232.

11. Personal interview with Paul Jones, Project Director, Community Youth Gang Services, South Central Los Angeles, April 1, 1993.

12. Useni Eugene Perkins, *Explosion of Chicago's Black Street Gangs: 1900 to Present* (Chicago: Third World Press, 1987), p. 79.

13. Fredric Dannen, "Revenge of the Green Dragons," *New Yorker* (November 16, 1992), pp. 76–99.

14. Brian McGrory, "5 Youths Shot in Lowell," *Boston Globe* (August 23, 1991), p. 63.

15. James Willwerth, "From Killing Fields to Mean Streets," *Time* (November 18, 1991), p. 103.

16. Mark S. Dunston, *Street Signs: An Identification Guide of Symbols of Crime and Violence* (Powers Lake, Wis.: Performance Dimension Publishing, 1992), pp. 47–48.

17. Michael Kronenwetter, *United They Hate: White Supremacist Groups in America* (New York: Walker and Company, 1992), pp. 77–80.

18. Jeanne Seligmann, "Mixed Messages," *Newsweek* (April 12, 1993), pp. 28–29.

19. David Ferrel, "8 High School Students Held in Rape, Assault Case," *Los Angeles Times* (March 19, 1993), pp. A1ff.

20. Jason Van Derbeken, "Complex dynamics shape local grafitti phenomenon," *The Daily News* (February 28, 1993), pp. A1ff.

21. Patricia Nalon, "Suburban Police Fear Gang Start-ups," *Boston Globe* (November 18, 1991), pp. A1+, 17.

22. "Gang membership," p. 1.

Chapter 4

1. Herbert Asbury, *The Gangs of New York: An Informal History of the Underworld* (New York: Knopf, 1927), p. 240.

2. Ibid. pp. 255–256.

3. Anne Campbell, *The Girls in the Gang* (New York: Basil Blackwell, 1991), pp. 12–13.

4. Ibid. pp. 13–14, 19.

5. Useni Eugene Perkins, *Explosion of Chicago's Black Street Gangs: 1900 to Present* (Chicago: Third World Press, 1987), p. 28.

6. Campbell, pp. 19–20.

7. W. B. Miller, "Violence by Youth Gangs and Youth Groups as a Crime Problem in Major American Cities," (Washington D.C.: U.S. Government Printing Office, 1975), as cited in Anne Campbell, *The Girls in the Gang*, p. 23.

8. J. Quicker, "The Chicana Gang: A Preliminary Description," paper delivered to the Pacific Sociological Association, San Jose (1974), as cited in Anne Campbell, *The Girls in the Gang*, pp. 25–26.

9. Anne Campbell, "Female Participation in Gangs," *Gangs in America*, ed. C. Ronald Huff (Newbury Park, Calif.: Sage Publications, 1990), pp. 178–180.

10. Campbell, *The Girls in the Gang*, p. 26.

11. James Hagedorn, *People and Folk, Gangs, Crime and the Underclass in a Rustbelt City* (Chicago: Lakeside Press, 1988), pp. 58, 192.

12. Joseph Bauer, ed., "Letters from a Teenage Jail," *Seventeen* (August 1991), pp. 238–239.

13. Michael Daly, "The Eleven Least Wanted," *New York* (October 21, 1991), pp. 18–20.

14. S. C. Gwynne, "Up from the Streets," *Time* (April 30, 1990), p. 34.

15. Laurie Becklund and Marc Lacey, "Homeboys Get Attention—Homegirls Just Get Babies," *Los Angeles Times* (March 15, 1993), pp. 2ff.

16. Laurie Becklund, "I Wanted Somebody to Love," *Los Angeles Times* (March 15, 1993), pp. E2ff.

17. Ibid. p. E2.

18. *Gangs, Crime and Violence in L.A., 1992,* (County of Los Angeles: Office of the District Attorney, May 1992), p. xiii.

Chapter 5

1. Adrian Walker and Charles A. Radin, "Of Violence and the Young," *The Boston Globe* (April 28, 1991), pp. A1ff.

2. James Hagedorn, *People and Folk, Gangs, Crime and the Underclass in a Rustbelt City* (Chicago: Lakeside Press, 1988), pp. 42–44.

3. Statistics from Los Angeles County Sheriff's Department's Operation Safe Streets, April 15, 1993.

4. Anne Campbell, *The Girls in the Gang* (New York: Basil Blackwell, 1991), p. 33.

5. Luis S. Rodriguez, *Always Running, La Vida Loca: Gang Days in L.A.* (Willamantic, Conn.: Curbstone Press, 1993), p. 250.

6. Jeff Kraner, "In L.A. Gangs, Bravado Bordering on Suicide," *The Boston Globe* (December 22, 1991), sec. 1, p. 2.

7. Walker and Radin, pp. A1ff.

8. Kenneth B. Clark, *Dark Ghetto, Dilemmas of Social Power* (New York: Harper and Row, 1965), p. 47.

9. Greg Barrios, "A Father's Gift," *Los Angeles Times* (March 31, 1993), pp. 1ff.

10. Martin Sanchez Jankowski, *Islands in the Street* (Berkeley: University of California Press, 1991), p. 185.

11. S.C. Gwynne, "Up from the Streets," *Time* (April 30, 1993), p. 34.

12. Ko-Lin Chin, "Chinese Gangs and Extortion," *Gangs in America*, ed. C. Ronald Huff (Newbury Park, Calif.: Sage Publications, 1990) p. 134.

13. Jeffrey Fagan, "New Facts about Urban Gangs," *The 1994 World Book Year Book, World Book Encyclopedia* (Chicago: World Book, Inc., 1994), p. 130.

Chapter 6

1. Jacob August Riis, *How the Other Half Lives* (New York: Hill and Wang, 1957), p. 170.

2. *Gang Prevention Through Targeted Outreach*, Boys and Girls Clubs of America, prepared under Grant No. 90-JD CX-K004 from the office of Juvenile Justice and Delinquency Prevention, Office of Justice Programs, U.S. Department of Justice, 1993, p. 11.

3. Ibid. pp. 9–10.

4. James Hagedorn, *People and Folk, Gangs, Crime and the Underclass in a Rustbelt City* (Chicago: Lakeside Press, 1988), p. 91.

5. Luis J. Rodriguez, *Always Running, La Vida Loca: Gang Days in L.A.* (Willamantic, Conn.: Curbstone Press, 1993), pp. 103–111.

6. Fredric Dannen, "The Revenge of the Green Dragons," *New Yorker* (November 16, 1991), pp. 77–78.

7. Ibid. pp. 80–81.

8. *Gang Prevention Through Targeted Outreach*, pp. 10–13.

9. Mark S. Dunston, *Street Signs: An Identification Guide of Symbols of Crime and Violence* (Powers Lake, Wis.: Performance Dimension Publishing, 1992), pp. 4–10.

10. Ibid. p. 28.

11. Terry Wilson, "Only the victim has a life sentence," *Chicago Tribune* (February 25, 1993), pp. A1ff.

12. Dannen, pp. 80–81.

13. William Gale, *The Compound* (New York: Rawson Associates, 1977), pp. 121–122.

14. Ibid. p. 28.

15. Personal interview with Sergeant Wes McBride, director of Operation Safe Streets, Los Angeles County Sheriff's Department, Los Angeles County, April 15, 1993.

16. *Gangs, Crime and Violence in L.A., 1992*, (County of Los Angeles: Office of the District Attorney, May 1992), p. xiii.

17. William Boyles, Jr., "American Scene: Letter from L.A.," *Esquire* (July 1992), pp. 37–38.

18. R. Lincoln Keiser, *The Vice Lords, Warriors of the Streets* (New York: Holt, Rinehart and Winston, 1969), pp. 29–30.

19. Joseph Bauer, ed., "Letters from a Teenage Jail," *Seventeen* (August 1991), p. 239.

20. Personal interview with Tammy Membreno, director of Barrio Action Group, Los Angeles, April 1, 1993.

21. "No Way Out," *Time* (August 17, 1992), pp. 28–40.

22. Jeff Kramer, "In L.A. Gangs, Bravado Bordering on Suicide," *The Boston Globe* (December 22, 1991), sec. 1, p. 2.

23. Tracy Wilkinson and Stephanie Chavez, "Elaborate Death Rites of Gangs," *Los Angeles Times* (March 2, 1992), pp. A1ff.

Chapter 7

1. John J. Goldman, "Gunman Kills Woman in Lobby of N.Y. Courthouse; Suspect Held," *Los Angeles Times* (February 24, 1991), p. A11.

2. Louise Kiernan, "Teen Killed Saying Goodnight," *Chicago Tribune* (March 22, 1993), sec. 1, p. 7.

3. Eric Eckholm, "Teen Age Gangs Are Inflicting Lethal Violence on Small Cities," *The New York Times* (January 31, 1993), pp. A1ff.

4. Richard C. Paddock, "Tahoe Towns Grapple With a Big City Problem—Gangs," *Los Angeles Times* (March 14, 1993), p. A3.

5. Jesse Katz, "County's Yearly Gang Death Toll Reaches 800," *Los Angeles Times* (January 19, 1993), pp. A1ff.

6. H. Range Hutson, Deirdre Anglin, and Michael J. Pratts, Jr., "Adolescents and Children Injured or Killed in Drive-By Shootings in Los Angeles," *The New England Journal of Medicine*, Vol. 330 (February 3, 1994), pp. 324–325.

7. Richard J. Lopez, "For City, One More Killing; For Family, Deepening Pain," *Los Angeles Times* (August 16, 1994), pp. A1, A22.

8. *Crime in the United States, Uniform Crime Reports* (Washington, D.C.: Federal Bureau of Investigation, 1992), pp. 279–283.

9. *Gangs, Crime and Violence in L.A., 1992*, (County of Los Angeles: Office of the District Attorney, May 1992), pp. xx–xxi.

10. Ibid.

11. Martin Sanchez Jankowski, *Islands in the Street* (Berkeley: University of California Press, 1991), p. 142.

12. Ibid. p. 139.

13. Ibid. pp. 145–146.

14. James Haskins, *Street Gangs Yesterday and Today* (New York: Hastings House, 1978), pp. 105–107.

15. Useni Eugene Perkins, *Explosion of Chicago's Black Street Gangs: 1900 to Present* (Chicago: Third World Press, 1987), pp. 38–39.

16. James Hagedorn, *People and Folk, Gangs, Crime and the Underclass in a Rustbelt City* (Chicago: Lakeside Press, 1988), p. 104.

17. *Gangs, Crime and Violence in L.A.*, p. xxv.

18. Patrick J. Meehan and Patrick W. O'Carroll, "Gangs, Drugs and Homicide in Los Angeles," *American Journal of Diseases of Children*, vol. 146 (June 1992), American Medical Association, pp. 685–688.

19. Hagedorn, pp. 103–105.

Chapter 8

1. Martin Sanchez Jankowski, *Islands in the Street* (Berkeley: University of California Press, 1991), p. 266.

2. Rita Kramer, *At a Tender Age, Violent Youth and Juvenile Justice* (New York: Holt, 1988), pp. 53, 63, 65–77.

3. Lois Smith Owens and Vivian Verdell Gordon, *Prisons and the Criminal Justice System* (New York: Walker, 1992), pp. 65–66.

4. Kurt Pizer, "Vital Volunteers," *Los Angeles Times* (May 15, 1993), pp. B1ff.

5. Jankowski, p. 270.

6. Owens and Gordon, pp. 34–36.

7. Ibid. pp. 18–22.

8. Ibid. pp. 88–91.

9. Bertha Davis, *Instead of Prison* (New York: Franklin Watts, 1986), pp. 91–95.

10. Owens and Gordon, p. 48.

11. Ibid. p. 51.

12. Tony Lesce, *The Big House: How America's Prisons Work* (Port Townsend, Wash.: Loopmanics Unlimited, 1991), pp. 25–26.

13. Ibid. p. 27.

14. *Corrections, Public Safety, Public Service* (California Department of Corrections, 1993), pp. 12–15.

15. Rene Hernandez, letter to author, May 9, 1993.

Chapter 9

1. Vicki Torres, "Three Young Murder Witnesses Learn the Price of Courage," *Los Angeles Times* (March 12, 1993), pp. A1ff.

2. "Gang Membership Crosses Cultural, Geographic Bounds," *School Safety Update* (November 1991), National School Safety Center News Service, p. 1.

3. Kate Shatzkin, "Protection for Rent," *Seattle Times/Post Intelligencer* (February 21, 1993), pp. A1ff.

4. Deborah Hasting, "Barricaded Streets: A Way to Lower Crime or Raise Property Values?" *Chicago Tribune* (February 7, 1993), pp. 18ff.

5. *Gang Prevention Through Targeted Outreach*, Boys and Girls Clubs of America, prepared under Grant No. 90-JD-CX-K004 from the office of Juvenile Justice and Delinquency Prevention, Office of Justice Programs, U.S. Department of Justice, 1993, pp. 74–75 and Fact Sheet.

6. Robbie Callaway and Roxanne Spillett, "Making a Difference in Public Housing," *Young People and America's Future*, quarterly bulletin to contributors, Boys and Girls Clubs of America (Summer 1991), p. 3.

7. Personal interview with Officer John Rozales, Community Relations, Northeast Division, Los Angeles Police Department, May 21, 1993.

8. John J. Goldman, "Teaching Young Offenders to Graduate from Crime," *Los Angeles Times* (February 9, 1993), pp. A1ff.

9. Ibid. pp. 14–15.

10. Jesse Katz, "Fighting to Keep a City's Soul," *Los Angeles Times* (December 31, 1992), pp. A1ff.

11. Lou Ranson, "Isiah Thomas' Mom, Subject of T.V. Film, 'A Mother's Courage,'" *Jet* (December 11, 1989), p. 36.

12. *General Information Guide*, Community Youth Gang Services, Los Angeles, April 11, 1991.

13. Seth Mydans, "Gangs Go Public in New Fight for Respect," *New York Times* (May 2, 1993), pp. 1ff.

14. Jesse Katz, "Making a Bed to End a Bloody Cycle," *Los Angeles Times* (August 27, 1992), pp. B1ff.

Glossary

bail—An amount of money or item of value that can be paid to the court so that a person charged with a crime can leave jail until the time he or she must appear in court. If the person does not appear in court at the scheduled time, the bail is taken by the court. Bail helps guarantee that the person will appear in court.

barrio—Spanish for neighborhood. Barrio or *varrio* also refers to a Chicano gang's territory.

Black Brotherhood—A gang made up of African-American prisoners.

Black Gangster Disciple Nation—A black Chicago gang whose symbol is crossed pitchforks and a six-pointed star. Members wear an earring in the right ear and tilt hats to the right.

Black Muslims—Members of the Nation of Islam, a Muslim religious group.

Black Panthers—A black activist group of the late 1960s and 1970s.

Bloods—A large African-American gang, active in the Los Angeles area. The Bloods began in Compton, California and are associated with the color red.

chicano—A term given to Mexican Americans during the 1970s.

cholo, chola—A member of a Mexican-American gang. A cholo is a male; a chola is a female. The term originated as the name for those who were unable to accept either Mexican- or Anglo-American values.

clique—A group with close ties, also known as a posse or crew.

cocaine—A narcotic derived from the leaves of the coca plant.

community—A group of people who share location, interests, and experiences. They agree upon leadership and rules that govern their responsibilities and obligations to one another.

community service—Acts of service to the community, often given as a sentence rather than prison as a form of punishment for lesser crimes or misdemeanors.

conviction—A decision made by the court, which could be the judge and the jury, that the defendant is guilty as charged.

crack—A highly addictive derivative of cocaine.

Crips—An African-American gang originating in Los Angeles. Crips allegedly received their name from the fact that they cripple enemies. They are associated with the color blue.

dai lo—Leader of a Chinese gang.

defendant—A person charged with a crime.

defense attorney—A lawyer who defends someone accused of an offense.

ethnic group—A group of people that come from the same country or share a common culture and heritage.

extortion—A demand for money using threats of violence.

felony—A serious crime, such as murder or armed robbery.

Folk Nation—A coalition of Chicago gangs that includes the Black Gangster Disciples and Spanish Cobras.

gang—A group that comes together with the primary purpose of performing illegal acts.

gangbanger—A gang member who will shoot enemies of the gang.

ghetto—A neighborhood where members of an ethnic group are forced to live.

graffiti—Stylized writing, usually on walls, that communicates meaning to gang members. It is used to mark out turf.

heroin—A highly addictive narcotic drug made from opium and usually injected.

homeboy, homegirl—A member of one's gang. Sometimes called "homie."

incarceration—Being in jail or prison as a result of a sentence for criminal activity.

inmate—A person imprisoned in a correction institution.

jump in, jump out—A jump in is a beating that a gang member undergoes in order to join a gang. A jump out is a beating for leaving the gang.

juvenile—A young person, usually under the age of eighteen.

marijuana—A drug made from the leaves of *Cannabis sativa*.

Mexican Mafia—The oldest and one of the largest prison gangs. It is also called *La Eme,* Spanish for "M."

misdemeanor—A minor offense. The penalty may be a fine, probation, or a short sentence in jail.

moniker —A street name by which a gang member is known. Hispanic gangs call their monikers *placas*.

pachuco—A term used in the 1930s and 1940s to refer to Mexican Americans who dressed in a distinctive style.

parole—Release before a prison sentence has been totally served. The person is then under supervision of a parole officer.

People—A coalition of Chicago gangs including the Vice Lords, El Rukn, and Latin Kings.

posse—A group often with a common interest, also known as a gang or clique.

prejudice—Prejudging someone on the basis of his or her ethnicity, race, sex, or religion.

probation—A sentence that does not result in a jail or prison term. The offender lives in the community under the supervision of a probation officer.

prosecutor—An attorney who represents the state in proceedings against a defendant.

public defender—An attorney paid for by the state to represent defendants who cannot pay for their own lawyers.

racism—Prejudice against a person or group based on race.

rumble—A fight between gangs.

self-esteem—A feeling of self-worth.

skinheads—White youth that dress in a distinctive manner, such as wearing heavy boots. Usually they shave their heads.

stereotype—A generally held belief about the behavior or characteristics of groups of people. Stereotypes can be positive or negative, but most of the time, they are negative.

tag—A graffiti signature.

tag banger—A member of a tagging crew or posse who carries weapons and engages in fights with other tagging groups or gangs.

tagbanging—Backing up a tag with violence.

tagger—A person who marks territory with graffiti. Although the activity is illegal, the person may or may not be a member of a gang.

vato—Dude or guy.

vato loco—A crazy dude or gang member with a street reputation.

wannabee—A person who wants to be a gang member.

White Aryan Resistance (W.A.R.)—A white supremacist movement organized by Tom Metzger, a white separatist.

White Aryan Resistance Youth—A branch of the White Aryan Resistance that tries to recruit skinheads.

wilding—A group assault or beating of an individual.

zoot suit—A fashion adopted by young Mexican Americans in the 1930s and 1940s. It consists of high-waisted baggy pants and a loose, wide-shouldered thigh-length jacket.

Further Reading

Nonfiction Books

Barden, Renardo. *The Facts About Gangs.* New York: Crestwood House, 1989.

Clark, Phyllis Elperin, and Robert Lehrman. *Doing Time, a Look at Crime and Prison.* New York: Hastings House, 1980.

Dunston, Mark S. *Street Signs, An Identification Guide of Symbols of Crime and Violence.* Powers Lake, Wis.: Performance Dimension Publishing, 1992.

Gardner, Sandra. *Street Gangs in America.* New York: Franklin Watts, 1992.

Greenberg, Keith Elliot. *Out of the Gang.* Minneapolis, Minn.: Lerner Publications, 1992.

Hagedorn, James M. *People and Folks, Gangs, Crime and the Underclass in a Rustbelt City.* Chicago: Lakeview Press, 1988.

Haskins, James. *Street Gangs Yesterday and Today.* New York: Hastings House, 1978.

Hoenig, Gary. *Reaper, the Story of a Gang Leader.* New York: Bobbs, Merrill, 1975.

Kronenwetter, Michael. *United They Hate, White Supremacist Groups in America.* New York: Walker and Company, 1992.

Owens, Lois Smith, and Vivian Verdell Gordon. *Prisons and the Criminal Justice System.* New York: Walker and Company, 1992.

123

Voices of Conflict, Teenagers Themselves. Compiled by Glenbard East Echo. Advised by Howard Spanogle. New York: Adams Books, 1987.

Webb, Margo. *Coping with Street Gangs.* New York: Rosen Publishing Group, 1990.

Fiction Books About Gangs and Gang Neighborhoods

Dunnahoo, Terry. *Who Cares About Espie Sanchez.* New York: Dutton, 1977.

Hinton, S.E. *The Outsiders.* New York: Viking Press, 1967.

—*Rumble Fish.* New York: Delacorte Press, 1976.

Hopper, Nancy J. *The Truth or Dare Trap.* New York: Dutton, 1985.

Le Voy, Myron. *Shadow Like a Tiger.* New York: Harper and Row, 1981.

Meyers, Walter Dean. *Scorpions.* New York: Harper and Row, 1988.

Murphy, Barbara. *Ace Hits Rock Bottom.* New York: Delacorte Press, 1985.

O'Dell, Scott. *Child of Fire.* Boston: Houghton Mifflin, 1974.

Peterson, P. J. *Nobody Else Can Walk It for You.* New York: Delacorte Press, 1982.

Spinelli, Jerry. *The Bathwater Gang.* Boston: Little Brown, 1990.

Articles

Bauer, Joseph, ed. "Letters from a Teenage Jail." *Seventeen* (August 1991), pp. 238–239.

Becklund, Laurie, and Marc Lacy. "Homeboys Get Attention—Homegirls Just Get Babies." *Los Angeles Times* (March 15, 1993), p. E2.

Daly, Michael. "The Eleven Least Wanted." *New York* (October 21, 1991), pp. 18–20.

Dannen, Frederick. "The Revenge of the Green Dragons." *New Yorker* (November 16, 1992), pp. 76ff.

Ecklholm, Eric. "Teen Age Gangs Are Inflicting Lethal Violence on Small Cities." *New York Times* (January 31, 1993), pp. A1ff.

Katz, Jesse. "Making a Bid to End a Bloody Cycle." *Los Angeles Times* (August 27, 1992), pp. B1ff.

Kramer, Jeff. "In L.A. Gangs, Bravado Bordering on Suicide." *Boston Globe* (December 24, 1991), sec. 1, p. 2.

Methvin, Eugene H. "When the Gangs Came to Tacoma." *Reader's Digest* (May 1992), pp. 134ff.

Mydans, Seth. "Gangs Go Public in New Fight for Respect." *New York Times* (May 3, 1993), pp. 1ff.

"No Way Out." *Time* (August 17, 1992), pp. 38–40.

Ranson, Lou. "Isiah Thomas' Mom, Subject of T.V. Film, 'A Mother's Courage.'" *Jet* (December 11, 1989), p. 36.

Walker, Adrian, and Charles A. Radin. "Of Violence and the Young." *Boston Globe* (April 28, 1991), pp. A1ff.

Wilkinson, Tracy, and Stephanie Chavez. "Elaborate Death Rites of Gangs." *Los Angeles Times* (March 2, 1992), pp. A1ff.

Willwerth, James. "From Killing Fields to Mean Streets." *Time* (November 16, 1992), pp. 103–105.

Index